Dedication:

This book is dedicated to my children
~ Alyssa, Kyl, Alex, and Gabriel ~
Thank you for raising me with Love

Go Gratitude!

Discover the Master Key that opens all doors of Possibility . . .
now present within YOU.

Stacey Robyn

www.ExpressGratitude.com
A Passalong Book

Go Gratitude!

Discover the Master Key that opens all doors of Posibility . . .

now present within YOU.

Stacey Robyn

Published by:
Pass Along Concepts
2305C Ashland St. #406
Ashland, OR 97520
http://www.PassAlongBooks.com

Cover Design:
Michael R. Boyce & Beril Ancel

Book Design:
Michael R. Boyce

ISBN 0-9754782-9-X

Printed in the United States of America

"To speak gratitude is courteous and pleasant, to enact gratitude is generous and noble, but to live gratitude is to touch Heaven."

~ Johannes A. Gaertner

TABLE OF CONTENTS

FOREWORD

I'm grateful to have met Stacey and Ken. It's not because they've blessed us with the opportunity to be a big part of the worldwide success of Go Gratitude, it's because Stacey and Ken are the total embodiment of their work and they make me, my wife Beril and my team here at Pass Along Concepts feel incredible. They shine with Gratitude; they are true walkers of what they are teaching. We learn from them every day as we help them spread this powerful message.

I remember the day I first talked to Stacey. She called my office telling me that she was excited about what we were doing here at Pass Along Concepts and that she had a vision to launch a program called Go Gratitude. Stacey and I had this instant connection because I had written a book on a topic that was similar, which was the one simple act of acknowledging people and how it could change our world. I instantly connected with her desire to get the message of Gratitude out into the world.

It was a brief conversation, but enough to know that we needed to meet to discuss this idea further. One week later my wife and I met Stacey and Ken in a small coffee shop up near Portland Oregon. We knew in that moment that there was something powerful going on. Intuition was screaming at us. I decided that no matter the results, I wanted to help them in any way I could to get Go Gratitude off the ground.

Do you want to know why Go Gratitude was so successful and powerful? It wasn't from anything we at Pass Along did. It wasn't the amazing flash movie Stacey co-created with Trevor Thomas. It wasn't the technology, the website, the cards or anything else. These certainly helped but I can boil it down to one thing . . .

It was Stacey and Ken's belief and knowingness that it would be huge. Period! It was their pure connection to Gratitude. To this day, even after hundreds of thousands of people have received their messages and Stacey becoming an overnight success as an author, they still hold this pure energy, this deep belief in what they are doing.

Boy, did I learn a lot from this. We all can!

I have seen more conviction and belief in their work than I have seen in best-selling successful, worldwide authors I have been known over the years. I think this is what over a half of million people who've been exposed to the Go Gratitude Experiment have also felt and one of the reasons why we connect with the messages. We have somehow tapped into the energy stream they released throughout the world, using technology, email, books, and cards but no matter what, an energy stream directly connected to them.

Their belief, strong yet free of expectation, is the exact reason why Go Gratitude is so powerful and impacting hundreds of thousands of lives right now. For being this strong, I am grateful to both of them. For being so gracious amidst such huge success, I am also grateful. I am grateful for the opportunity to play with Stacey and Ken and especially to publish this incredible book. I am grateful we've had the opportunity to weave together Go Gratitude and the Pass Along Concept. I am grateful for the thousands and thousands of messages we've received and the excitement that has been expressed to us around this book.

Remember, this is just the experiment part of Go Gratitude. We have just begun and I believe this book and all the things it offers will touch millions of lives. Thank you for being one of them. Thank you Stacey and Ken. You two are awesome! I love you!

Go with Gratitude.

Robert Evans
Founder of Pass Along Concepts
Ashland, Oregon

Go Gratitude!

INTRODUCTION

I am soooooooo excited you are here!

A power now lies within you, waiting for your recognition, your call, your direct attention to spring to life and deliver whatever your pure heart desires.

Synchronistically . . .

You've just embarked on a universally unique adventure, experimenting with intentionally using the Master Key of Gratitude to unleash this source force within, giving life to your dreams, power to your passions, and prosperity to your pursuits!

Allow me now to give you a bit of insight on how Go Gratitude came to be. In the Spring of 2005, I took a 42 day retreat to clear my head, inspire my soul, and clarify my plans for pursuing a passionate life. My retreat was a spur of the moment decision, so I sent a quick note to friends and family, letting them know my plans for the next 6 weeks, and that something "big! Big! BIG!" was coming. I remember feeling excited, wondering what 'big! Big! BIG!' really meant.

During these 6 weeks I daily dedicated time to honor my creativity, indulging in all sorts of artistic outlets such as drawing, painting, cloud gazing, and a whole lot of doodling.

Doodling? Well, yes. It's a favorite pastime of mine.

By releasing any expected outcome, I simply allow my creativity to flow freely – just me, the pen, and all possibility! One evening, while musing on my doodles, I noted that many commonly recognized symbols were peeking through my orderly disorder.

And then, as if arranged by fate, I asked my Sweetheart, "What is the symbol for Gratitude?" Think about it. There's a symbol for the sun, the moon, love, peace – even a simple "swoosh" is recognizable world-wide. There must be a symbol for Gratitude!

...and Voila! I glanced down to witness this symbol of Gratitude being created by my very own hand. Immediately, I glimpsed a little 'g' in a circle. 'Gratitude begins with a G', I thought. Perfect! (I still get chills thinking about it! Wow!)

Well, let me tell you – between then and now I have witnessed a myriad of messages and confirmations revealed by this simple symbol, that prove beyond a doubt that Gratitude is everywhere. Many of these are revealed in the "42 Knew Views on Gratitude" series – and I'm sure many, many more will emerge as creative minds converge to explore, expand and experiment with Gratitude.

Now I must confess . . .

I'd been drawing this symbol for weeks. I had it 'on the brain' you might say. It was fun to draw, all whirly-swirly and a challenge to get it JUST RIGHT. I suppose this fascination allowed me to easily recognize it when I finally thought to ask.

Can you say Divine providence? Serendipity? Magic?
Perhaps all three!!!

Now, you might ask, "Why Gratitude? Where did this inquiry spring from?" It may seem random, and yet there is a beginning to all things. Dr. Masaru Emoto was my Gratitude Muse. You may be familiar with Dr. Emoto's work with water crystals, and the effect thoughts and words have on their physical structure.

While relishing his awe-inspiring book, "The Hidden Messages in Water," I came upon an idea that will forever change my life, and perhaps yours, as well.

Dr. Emoto believes that Gratitude is a gift of Love; it is what Love returns to the world, as a symbol of appreciation for life, for being, for NOW. Dr. Emoto also feels that the "Love and Gratitude" water crystal is the most beautiful of all, for it exemplifies our highest nature, as Divine Creators.

As I pondered this possibility, a wave rippled through me with force, passion, and understanding. Immediately I envisioned a wake of Gratitude rolling across our planet, re-connecting our water bodies to Love. Passed person to person, heartbeat by heartbeat, this wake would roll through our bodies – mostly water – to create a massive tide of change by simply focusing on Gratitude.

A vision to behold, indeed.

Quickly, I began to visualize what this wave might LOOK like, size-wise. So I put a number to it – one million people. Here are a few calculations for you:

(Remember – on average, our bodies are 70% water)

One gallon of water weighs: 8.33 pounds
Approx water weight of 150 lb. person: 105 pounds
Gallons of water, per 150 lb person: 12.61

This means one million people gathered in Gratitude will create a 12.61 million gallon wave of water, weighing an impressive 105 million pounds, rolling across planet Earth.

No devastation, no destruction . . . just Love and Gratitude invisibly waking at the heart of humanity.

Now – a wake of Gratitude connecting one million people is big! Big! BIG! I was beginning to catch a glimpse of my path, a passionate possibility fueling my inner fires crying 'yes! Yes! YES! This is it! This is what I've been asking for!'

By simply sharing this concept, this gift, this Master Key with friends and family alike, YOU will be increasing the momentum of this experiment, while simultaneously tapping into a collective power growing greater with every person, because it springs from the love of Gratitude. Now let's turn to science journalist and author Malcolm Gladwell for some insight on why this goal of one million is possible.

In his ground-breaking book The Tipping Point, Gladwell explores why change happens so quickly, and the patterns driving each shift. The tipping point is defined as the moment of critical mass, where a small change tips the scales and large effects are experienced. He points out that once you become aware of the patterns of change, you will begin to see them everywhere. Just like Gratitude.

Gladwell also explores personality types that drive social change — defining what he calls Connectors and Mavens. This experiment is growing and flowing rapidly because our gathering is filled with exactly these types of people – those who recognize an extraordinary idea and those who are widely connected to quickly pass along the message. This includes YOU!

Give yourself some well earned credit, as we have accomplished something previously unheard of ; purely, by word-of-mouth, we are creating a world wide wake of Gratitude! (With some help from technology, divine timing, and a sincere belief that one person does make a difference!)

Shall we add in another dimension?

Dr. David Hawkins, in his book Power vs. Force, concludes: "We all float on the collective level of consciousness of (hu)man kind, so that any increment we add comes back to us." Additionally, Hawkins relates that one person who chooses to live with optimism and non-judgment of others offsets the energy of 90,000 individuals vibrating at lower energetic frequencies. These impressive numbers are further multiplied by those who live in Love, Peace and Gratitude.

By Hawkins' calculations approximately 72,500 people are required to shift our mass consciousness into a state of peace and well being. Now imagine 1,000,000 hearts connected in Love and Gratitude. Wow!

I am deeply honored and filled with profound Gratitude to be here with You as we embark on a journey that will deeply affect countless lives, alter the way we view our world, and open all doors of possibility!

All together Now. . .   Go Gratitude!

MASTER KEY
LESSON 1

Symbols are keys to universal doors
passing through the conscious to the super-conscious
by embodying patterns of nature.

Gratitude is the Master Key opening passage for
Opportunity, Abundance, and Celebration.

Now witness this, as it is written in the Gratitude symbol:

egg = gestation = opportunity
spiral = growth = abundance
circle = completion = celebration

Go Gratitude!

Imagine being given a master key, yours for all eternity,
to open all doors of possibility. Rejoice, for it is so!

"I just wanted to say something on symbols. They are
keys to a universal language that unlock doors.
Don't worry if you do not know how to use the symbol.

The knowledge will come when you are ready for it .
Your guides will lead you to it.
I suggest taking the symbol, and meditating with it this week.
There is no wrong way to use it."
Love,
~ Carol Tessier

—UNITY SHAMBALLA GROUP

The Master Key resonates with me for many reasons. The first and biggest reason is the shape. I am a tie-dye artist and the most common tie-dye is a spiral design, a design that vibrates between the alpha and the omega of the universe. When I do my art, I let go and let the Divine flow through me. This design is based on Sacred Geometry and the Divine quotient, as is your design. (Holy is as Holy does.)

The second resonance of your design reminds me of my youth, some thirty years past. I used to surf and when I did I felt so alive. This was years before my personal transformation at a time when I was unread and had little experience. Your design reminds me of the green room; a place that all surfers yearn to be. Another name for the green room is 'tube ride,' that ultimate experience of spirit and wave. I didn't know it then, but surfing is one of the truest moments of NOW that a person can have. Every second is fluid and can change in an instant. There are no thoughts only reaction to the continuously advancing vibrations which are never the same twice. In those days when people asked me if I went to Church; I said yes and told them my Church was in the waves for it was in those moments of no-time that I felt the Divine presence. I didn't have to have Faith or Belief because I Knew. Living in the moment can do that for us humans because experience can transcend the ego mind. Even though I was experiencing the Divine I did not learn love and gratitude at that time. My remembrance still awaited me.

... Since I share your passion in forging a new world paradigm I will be a willing accomplice in planting this most Holy seed of Gratitude. I Know this one, it really works for me; in fact it releases the flood of bliss that is my life. Thank you for sharing this piece of yourself. I know many Conscious people who will love the work that you have done. Bless You.

Namaste,
~ Bruce

DRAW
LESSON 2

How to draw Gratitude?

and like this

Simple, easy, and wow! Now, go ahead –
take a few minutes to spin a bit of Gratitude.

As you enjoy the process
note how
mood, balance, flow and attention
Will affect how Gratitude appears.

So it IS in all matters.

Go Gratitude!

Be careful ~
You may find yourself doodling Gratitude everywhere musing
"There's just something about this symbol that
draws me in . . ."

"Doodling allows the unconscious to render in symbolic
expression. Symbols have universal as well as
personal meaning.

When you are stuck for an answer to a problem or looking for
creative innovation, the technique of doodling will unleash the
hidden symbolic powers of the unconscious mind. . .

Some people are prolific doodlers when they are talking on the
telephone, sitting at a meeting, attending a lecture or sitting in
any passive environment.

This doodling can reveal important and profound information
about how the person was feeling at the time, or, according
to Jung, latent emotional conflicts or unexpressed feelings.
In truth, no one can interpret our doodling except ourselves.
Though certain symbols appear to have universal applications
in the deep collective unconscious, how we experience these
symbolic expressions in our own life is unique to each of
us. Your subconscious mind is attempting to contact you all
the time. It is usually blocked by habitual conscious thought

patterns or emotions. It can also be drowned out by the mundane mental trivia that we repeatedly hash over. Learn to allow its conscious expression,
preferably every day."

http://enchantedmind.com/html/creativity/techniques/art_ of_doodling.html

Hello in gratitude, I am a teacher at the elementary level. Every morning, beside the date on the board, I put the sign Gratitude. Students (grade 6) started to ask me what it meant — so I explained to them that every time I felt gratitude, I put it there. They started to do the same. At the end of the day, we have a lot of Gratitude signs on the board.

Thank you
~ Rita

EFFECT
LESSON 3

Every breath,
as Word or wonder-ous sigh,
precipitates change.

Now
imagine our bodily waters flowing,
breath by breath,
covering all Creation in a mist of intentioned time.

As focus goes so will Creation flow.

Go Gratitude!

Breathe easily,
releasing vaporized sighs of matters realized thru intentioned
Gratitude.
ah – uh – mmmmmmm

Breath contains both air and moisture. The moisture,
or water, is impregnated and charged with the flowing

magnetism of feelings that attracts that which has been willed, visualized, and thought into form. Even the smallest amount of charged water has the ability to change all water that it comes into contact with. On the out breath, the moisture in the breath is in immediate contact with the moisture in the air of the macrocosm, and this magnetism ripples out to the entire Unified Field of magnetic energy in the astral plane.

8 degrees Leo – The Angels of Breath message,
also known as
The Angels of 'Romasara':
~ Spiritus Sanctus

www.spiritussanctus.com

...I am 38 and I am so grateful for the people who I am choosing to share my life with. I am experiencing a few important pivotal moments right now.

I have felt what it is like to stand in my own truth and feel authentic at a soul-full level for the first time really in my life!! When I do my guided visualizations, I breath in the most pure healing white light and see and feel it expanding from around my body all the way out into the world and into infinity.

I know that energy does permeate others at a soulful level. It feels sooo amazing and the more I do this the stronger it gets. Just think if we all did this at the same time one night for ten mins.??

Just think of how much soulful consciousness we can raise and the immediate effects of that!! WOW!! Thank you for reading my gratefuls.

~ Brad

CRYSTAL CLEAR
LESSON 4

Water crystals reveal structural alterations
bent by vibration, being currently
arranged to display Now.

Love beats true
within waking waters of time
called You and I.
Masterfully guided through Gratitude
this Source force Will create
bodies bent on behaving with
benevolent intentions
designed
to
witness Life as waking Art.

Go Gratitude!

Imagine a wake of Gratitude, flowing across every beating
heart, re-connecting our water bodies to Love.
Emoto – Grab your microscope.

Interview with Dr. Masaru Emoto on Gratitude:

REIKO: Have you come across a particular word or phrase
in your research that you have found to be most helpful in
cleaning up the natural waters of the world?

DR. EMOTO: Yes. There is a special combination that seems
to be perfect for this, which is love plus the combination
of thanks and appreciation reflected in the English word
gratitude. Just one of these is not enough. Love needs to
be based in gratitude, and gratitude needs to be based in
love. These two words together create the most important
vibration. And it is even more important that we understand
the value of these words.

For example, we know that water is described as H2O. If we
were to look at love and gratitude as a pair, gratitude is the
H and love is the O. Water is the basis that not only supports
but also allows the existence of life. In my understanding of
the concept of yin and yang, in the same way that there is one
O and two Hs, we also need one part yang/love to two parts
yin/gratitude, in order to come to a place of balance in the
equation.

———

. . . Once long ago, in 2002 probably, I was following my Soul's
command to give up all my life in England and go to Israel, and
a week before was meditating with an ancient tree asking it to
help me to bring Love to Israel's strife torn peoples. After a while
of patiently helping me, this voice came into my head from the
tree, saying:

"You know we don't need to go on sending Love, the world is full of Love, Israel too is full of Love, what we need to do is to teach people to receive the Love that is already here"

So learning to receive Love has been a strong part of my Love workshops ever since, and it is true, we don't receive loving energy easily, so many people have resistance to the idea that they are worthy, that they deserve to receive Love, and anyway they are too busy giving Love to find the time to receive it. Gratitude is of the same energy as Love, it is in the divine gift too, and again, everyone is happy to give Gratitude, but it is so important to learn to receive Gratitude from others, to Allow them to Love and Appreciate us with their Gratitude, so I add a word here, and say "Please dear (insert your name), open your hearts now, and receive my Gratitude for this wonderful expression of Joy you have given to me; in your heart say 'Yes, I am open to . . . Love & Gratitude and allow it to soak into your cells, twinkling as it goes."

With Love & Best Wishes
. . . from Bill
www.the-healer.co.uk

LUCID GRATITUDE
LESSON 5

Consciously directing attentions to Gratitude
during transition from Waking reality to Dream space
will create a bridge allowing intentional exploration,
Divine communion,
and passage to enlightening adventures.

Here is how:

1. Tonight, as you lie to rest, focus on Gratitude.
2. Imagine this symbol over your heart.

3. With each peaceful beat calming waters within,
feel a drift into sleep,
flowing knowing going is NOW -
resting on a ring of Gratitude,
leisurely floating Rivers of Abundance.
Rest. Soak. Splash.
Explore shores for treasures galore.
Prepare to wake in Gratitude.

Go Gratitude!

To activate Will during sleep excursions,
summon a symbol of Gratitude.
You will immediately connect with choice, awareness, and
power!

plus – flying remains an exhilarating option.

"Lucid dreams are also symbolic – yet in quite a different way,
– Their symbolism takes the form of beautiful landscapes
. . . different luminous phenomena, sunlight, clouds, and
especially a deep blue sky.
In a perfect instance of the lucid dream I float through
immensely wide landscapes,
with a clear blue, sunny sky, and a feeling of deep bliss
and Gratitude,
which I feel impelled to express by eloquent words of
thankfulness and piety.
Sometimes these words seem to me a little rhetorical,
but I cannot help it, as it is very difficult in dreams to control
emotional impulses –
Sometimes I conceive of what appears as a symbol, warning,
consoling, approving.

Flying or floating may be observed in all forms of dreams,
except perhaps the class of general dream sensations;
yet it is generally an indication that lucid dreams are coming."

—excerpt, A Study of Dreams by Frederik Van Eeden

. . . I love the messages, I am SO GRATEFUL for this opportunity and for you and how you are making all this possible-and I so appreciate how you use the language to express the situations-I can't express how much this means to me and how I'm enjoying it-shifting my thinking from the past into the present, and future, is just the beginning-I'm dreaming again, and perhaps best of all I'm getting unstuck from a situation that has held me captive for far, far too long and run my life for even longer.

Freedom to breathe, to feel joy, to celebrate, thank you, thank you, thank you-most of all for reminding me of who I really am and for reminding me of the celebration my life can be! This morning I awoke knowing today was a new beginning, and so it is and it is so.

I've long known that gratitude was both the greatest attitude and the most powerful energy on the planet, now being reminded of it is empowering and inspirational too! This is a great way to begin a New Year and new life!

In Light, Love, and Peace,
~ Amrita

BE A WAKE
LESSON 6

As surely as Gratitude returns to Self,
intentioned happynings manifest quickly.

Watch for unexpected, serendipitous sequences of events to
wake, roll and buoy current excursions.

In other words:

Imagine clearly. Love dearly. Go Gratitude.
Let everything else roll bye.

Go Gratitude!

By waking in Gratitude our water bodies will peacefully
shift to NOW realities ~ a circular 'see' of possibilities ~
being quickened past light speed, happyning ever so surely.
all is (s)well = waking gratitude

"Consider This: Revise the words, "Thank you,"
in your internaldictionary. Call upon these words to establish

deep awareness of how
your spirit touches others and how the good intentions of
others
stream energy into your experience. Wake up every time you
say, "Thank you." Say, "Thank you," often.

Thanking Yourself
Here's a less used phrase. Saying, I thank me,
to yourself
means, "I thank myself." Although you may not be in the habit
of
acknowledging your own efforts with Gratitude, it
strengthens your
energetic field when you do."

~ the Yoga of Alignment

Participating in Go Gratitude has taken my life to a whole
new level. Although I had practiced gratitude for many years,
this project brought it alive for me every day. I am cultivating a
garden of gratitude in my mind and my heart. And the results are
amazing. Every day gets better and better. I have gone through
some tough times recently with major struggles in relationships,
finances, health – every aspect of my life, really. The daily
gratitude messages kept me going and brightened some days
that were truly dark for me. Now the tide is turning and I feel the
wave of gratitude coming back to me.

Thank you, Thank you, Thank you for doing this work
~ Pamela O.

P.I.N.S. AND NEEDLES

LESSON 7

Remember the last time a hand or foot woke up?
Blood rushing, pins and needles.
Temporary, though none-the-less painful.

At times, this is
what happens with NOW awareness
as it floods into our waking reality,
seeking ports for universal understanding,
while naturally creating pressure at point of reception.
Temporary, though none-the-less painful.

Below is a formula for moving thru
moments of waking pains:

1. *P*ractice patience

2. *I*nspire creativity

3. *N*urture Love

4. *S*how Gratitude

" needles" to say, this works as well as You.
Let Love guide you through

to find peace
in this gathered wisdom.

Go Gratitude!

P.I.N.S. and Needles are physical signals
to alter current position in favor of waking Now.
Remember − this too will pass thru.

Awakening is a flowering of your innermost being.
It is a revelation of your essence,
hidden by long eons of self-delusion,
ignorance,
unbounded desires.
Enlightenment is an ending as well as a beginning:
the ending of the old, veiled, dark ego,
its longings, illusions, frustrations;
the beginning of a vast expanse,
an infinite field of the Unknown,
an adventure in consciousness.
It is a revolution:
it represents danger to the old way of life,
to old ways of thinking and living.
It is freedom from the known and the unknown;
from the real and the unreal;
from any appearance of division between you and Truth.

It is the abandoning of beliefs, dis-beliefs,
presumptions and stances,
self, ego,

call it what you will,
or call it nothing,
what it is.

It is the Path of the golden Dawn,
the Path out of the Night of Time
into the Bursting daylight of Eternal Now –
~ Petros

This has been a transforming experience – in thinking upon
the Gratitude . . . and all it's inspirations, I've seen people
and things differently. So much, that it's inspired a theory of
tolerance that for me must begin before gratitude can flow in
it's full integrity.

The D concept:

DIFUSE . . . DEFINE . . . DIRECT . . .

Diffuse emotional angst, define the source of the problem (or
fear), direct energy to a better place. All this inspired from the
P.I.N.S. and needles section of Gratitude.

Thanks and let everyone know that the D concept works – I
should know, I'm Dana. I made it up and it works for me. My
friends here in NYC are already adopting it.

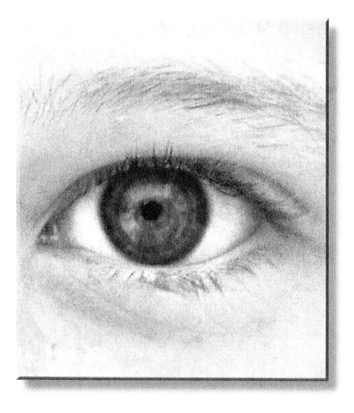

ALPHA AND OMEGA
LESSON 8

Gratitude begins with G
and ends with

e.

Mirror images of one another,
ALPHA AND OMEGA
are the beginning and ending of all creation.

Notice, I is centered in grat-I-tude –
All by Divine Design, of course.

Go Gratitude!

Gratitude kindly shifts our awareness to a circular
perspective,

being transparently aware of what's beyond the bend –
a glimpse beyond now by mirroring ends!

Ooohhh – let the chills move up your spine,
tingling truthfully as past notions fade, opening space
for everything between Alpha and Omega.

I am Alpha and Omega, the beginning and the ending, sayeth
the Lord, which is, and which was, and which is to come, the
Almighty.
Revelation 1.8

It is here in Revelation 1 –
the first chapter of the last book - that we meet the first
and last letters of the Greek alphabet The beginning and
the end are united in the Alpha Omega as a symbol of the
Everlasting God. The integration goes deeper with the
verse index corresponding to the (small) values
of the Letters Alpha and Omega.
They are calculated by summing the digits of the
Base Ten representation of the Number. These are also known
as the digital roots. Thus, the Numbers 1 and 8 – the digital
roots of Alpha and Omega –
give the index of their debut in Scripture in Revelation
1.8, which means that the revelation of the
divine title Alpha Omega is integrated with the numerical
values of the letters
(where RC indicates the Reduction Class value):
Revelation (1, 8) = Revelation (AlphaRC, OmegaRC)
The Alpha and Omega are intimately associated
with the Creator. As discussed at length in the article called
Gematria, these letters are numerically equivalent to the

Greek phrase "The Creator."

We have the identity:
Alpha + Omega = 801 = The Creator ( )

source: http://www.biblewheel.com/InnerWheels/
Revelation/Rev01.asp

. . . This year I have been on a journey. A journey from Lost to Found. I am 27. This year I have gone through the end of one long term relationship and the start of a brand new one – the one with myself. For months I have been on such a roller coaster. At times I have felt that I was floating in a bubble high above everything. Othertimes I've felt like I was drowning in the lowest cavern of the deepest sea. I've spent a lot of time mourning; the loss of my relationship, family, friends, things, lifestyle. Everything.

At the same time I have been grateful for the absolute wonder, peace and excitement of finding myself and 'waking up into my own life.'

Today, however, I felt a shift. Today, I realized that instead of mourning everything I have lost, I can be grateful that they were in my life. As a result, I realized that these things will always be a part of my life, **because I have gratitude for them.**

As I sat and thought of all of the gratitude I have for these people and these experiences, the most wonderful energy swept through my whole body. I couldn't move. All I could do was cry. My tears were those of joy and love and gratitude. And for the first time, as I noticed the energy I was feeling, I realized that I wasn't floating or sinking this time. This time what I felt was grounded. I felt that I was a part of the earth. In fact, I felt a part of everything.

I thank you for your gift of gratitude. It has changed my life in ways I could never have imagined. I also know that through this gift, I have, in turn, given it to others and will continue to do so.

Thank you. I am centered in Gratitude.

With Love, Light and Gratitude,
~ Oksana

SPEED
LESSON 9

Speed of nerve impulse = 136 meters per second
Speed of sound = 340.29 meters per second
Speed of light = 186,000 miles per second
Speed of thought = will
Speed of intention = discipline
Speed of acceptance = grace
Speed of release = compassion
Speed of Love = You Speed of Gratitude = Now

Go Gratitude!

Various time-frames give boundary,
insight, and relation.
'Multi-ness,' one may say.
Enjoy!
Be excellent!
Party on!

. . . In other words, though invisible to the human eye,
we seem to be immersed in a sort of universal ocean of

interconnectivity. Just as all creatures in a sea are connected by the cohesive body of water, so the entire world/universe is interconnected in a kind of cohesive psychic sea. There is nothing to which you are not attached in some way.

Evidently, even our thoughts are not just isolated ideas waiting to be acted upon, but are actually linked in some fashion to the object(s) of the thought. Sheldrake goes on to say, (1) "Our intentions stretch out into the world around us, and also extend into the future. We are linked to our environment and to each other." If, as Sheldrake says, we are linked to the future, then our thoughts effect what is coming. This means that our mental intentions, or stretching our thoughts outward, actually link to objects and draw them toward us.

With kindest regards,
~ Barry Carter

During this period of time my life has changed significantly, and the 42 (messages) I received from you often corresponded with moments where I needed that exact advice at that exact moment. For example, one night I had a particularly transformative experience wherein I went to a gathering of people in Toronto, Ontario and your (message) had given me some advice that included "Party on!" just at the moment I was feeling worried about going to this party due to my shyness and fear of dancing in front of people.

Well, a little boy I met that day that I was playing with (his mother is my close friend) showed me how to just let go and be yourself, and then I got that (message), which really showed me that the universe was telling me to just let go and party! That night I danced for the first time like no one was watching :)

... your (message) today comes at a particularly wonderful time, when I was exploring the nature of my self, and really trying to get in touch with who I am — realizing that I am the observer and decision maker, but that I am so much more, and I have to take that into account before I am able to lovingly rearrange the splintered aspects of my personality. Well, again, thank you for everything. I am touched by your loving energy.

~ Trent R.

DON'T PANIC
LESSON 10

In
T.H.H.G.T.T.G.
~ the Hitch Hikers Guide to the Galaxy ~
you will remember
our planet comes
due to be demolished by way of legislation.
Blown up. Bye-bye. Hasta la seeya.
Sound familiar?

Don't panic.

You Will witness worlds dissolving to reveal
alternative realities happyning Now.

Remember ~
Time is Now to govern self as sovereign State of Gratitude,
for our coming transition will happen
as surely as finding Self in knew territory.

It's all good.

Go Gratitude!

T.H.H.G.T.T.G.
records a tale of a universal computer
returning this answer: '42'.

as in THE answer.
to THE question.
you know the one.

Knew views on Gratitude x 42, eh?
Of course.

———

"When you accept changes in your sovereign reality
as the shifting persona of the Universal Soul,
you live in greater harmony with life itself.
Life becomes an exchange of energy between you
and the Universal Soul that is allowed to play out;
without judgment, and is experienced without fear.
This is the underlying meaning of unconditional love:
to experience life in all its manifestations as a single,
unified intelligence that responds perfectly to the
projected image of each soul.

It is for this reason that when you project Gratitude tothe
Universal Soul,
regardless of circumstance or condition,
life becomes increasingly supportive in opening you
to activate your divine imprints.
This feeling of Gratitude coupled with the mental
concept of appreciation is expressed like an invisible message
in all directions and at all times.

In this particular context, gratitude to the Universal Soul
is the overarching motive behind all forms of expression
to which humanity aspires.

Every breath, every word, every touch, every thought, every
thing
is centered on expressing this sense of Gratitude;
a Gratitude that you are sovereign and supported by a
Universal Soul
that expresses itself through all forms and manifestations of
intelligence
with the sole objective of creating the ideal reality
to activate your divine imprints
and transform your entire being into Divine Essence.

It is this specific form of Gratitude that accelerates
the activation of your divine imprints
and their peculiar ability to integrate the disparate
components
of your body, mind, heart, and soul, and to transform them
to the state of perception and expression of Divine Essence –.
Establishing a relationship with the universe
through the outflow of Gratitude
also attracts life experience that is trans formative -
experience that is richly devoted to uncovering life's
deepest meaning and most formative purpose."
~ Wingmakers

Today's Go Gratitude brought to mind George Bush. While I
definitely would not vote for him, what came to mind was the
personal attacks that are coming to him and the example that
we can learn from. I was reminded that he is both divine and

human. Let us wish him peace, love, joy. I am grateful for the
mirror he provides. He is our Brother.

Go Gratitude!
~ Elizabeth

FLUSH WITH FOCUS
LESSON 11

Meditation is a single point of focus.

Simplify by choosing Gratitude to shift current focus into
a pure, nothing-is-everything-is-something state of awareness,
allowing feelings to flow, gracefully immersing Self into NOW.

Intentionally create in vivid detail every aspect of Gratitude.
See it from multi-verses,
beyond centered nothing-ness
to exist at being
imagined
by
YOU.

As distractions surface,
flush through Gratitude
returning Lovingly to Source
as Gifts of NOW.

Just and pure.

Go Gratitude!

Those distractions?

Wish-ing away.
Down the bowl. Flush, flush.
Grateful to know you – done your job, now bye-bye.
Closing the lid. Stepping away. Later.

Spiritus Sanctus writes:

"When a person uses the power of their quadrapolar magnet,
the fourfold power of
desire, thought, flowing feeling, and sensation to
seek (Gratitude) above all else,
these powers penetrate through veils of obscurity and
distraction
and attune the individual consciousness to Divine
Consciousness and Feeling.
where the attention goes, energy flows."

If a person focuses on the problem itself and continues to give
it powerful
mental and emotional energy, especially if the mental and
emotional energy
is negative, then the quadrapolar magnet creates attracts
exactly what is not wanted.
By focusing on (Gratitude) instead, at the same time that the
problem is being
confronted, a person connects to Omnipresent, All powerful,
and All knowing Divine Mind and Feeling, and to the
heavenly hosts.
In this way help and instruction is attracted, manifesting

solutions to any and all situations.
In attuning to Divine Mind, the Theta brainwave state of deep
inner thought
opens the Book of Life and regains understanding of the
original purity of all ideas.
Gifts of eloquence, artistic talent, clairvoyance and other
occult powers are regained.
"All that I do ye shall do and more."
Once (Gratitude) is found through one pointed focus of the
powers
of consciousness and feeling, all other gifts and delights are
added in a way that is in the highest good of all. we are one
(in Gratitude)."

~ Spiritus Sanctus

. . . I have been experiencing an amazing opening of creativity
and possibility in my life in the past 3 weeks after an incredible
experience of gratitude. A huge internal shift has allowed me to
connect with so many people and to find the possibility of love
and connection with everyone I come into contact with. People I
sit next to on the airplane, bus, in lines, on the sidewalk.

The pivotal experience was during my tai chi class. During
the tai chi form, I felt a great warmth and feeling of love and
gratitude for everyone who has touched my life and helped me
on my journey of healing from a severe depression 2 1/2 years
ago. I ended in a standing meditation with tears of joy running
down my cheeks. I sensed a deep sadness in the room from
another class member. He shared with us that he was feeling
very distraught. I offered to give him a touch.

After placing my hands on his shoulders, waves of emotion poured through me in the form of sighs, then sobs, then wails and cries from the depths of my soul. It was as though the grief of the world was passing through me. I stayed in light touch with my friend throughout the sounding. He had joined me in releasing with sound. Our breaths calmed and we were able to look into each others eyes with deep compassion.

When I returned home, I had to write in my journal to release an outpouring of thoughts and feelings. I have continued to write, talk with loved ones and to try to be with this amazing sense of energy and life force. All my spiritual guides, friends, have advised me to give space to this opening, to let it take shape without forcing or trying to make anything happen. I am trusting that I will be guided to follow the lead of the voice within. I get it.

The gratitude allowed me to release many layers of emotional holding and to let the creative force of the universe to pass through me. It is such a gift.

~ Marilyn

QUICKENING
LESSON 12

Notice presently amplified power
to draw intentioned events to Now.

This is hour Quickening,
an opening to manifest choice,
revealing our creative-ness
as present, powerful and ever-so-potent.

Remember:
in order to thrive,
allow Self to be guided by Gratitude.
Be clear, concise and collectively aware.

Simply
appreciate and ye shall receive –
Quickly.

Go Gratitude!

hooray!

let us give thanks for this
'serendipitous-by-choice – of-passionate-nature'
gathering of Gratitude,
witnessing collective change   x 42 days !!!

~ Namaste.

* The resonance of Earth (Schumann Resonance)
has been 7.8Hz for thousands of years. Since 1980 it has risen
to over 12Hz.
This means that 16 hours now equate to a 24 hour day. Time is
speeding up!

~ Gregg Braden

Thank you for including the SNAIL!
I think they've always known about Gratitude, and the
Quickening . . . this is why they are happy to take their
time, and carry the symbol of life of their shells.
Oh, every time I meditate on the gratitude symbol before
sleep . . . my dreams are filled with wonder and water.
When I forget to do this, I don't dream!

Fondly,
~ Snaili

NOTE OF GO
LESSON 13

All notes recorded in Gratitude
will energetically gather
as saving Grace for
up-coming opportunities to play.

Record daily Gratitude as matter of discipline ,
cultivating safe haven for
Now aligned
happynings, harbingers and ground crew alike.
Consider wisely
true matters at heart,
as time will remember Now hence.

Go Gratitude!

By recording Gratitude Now, You Will
instantly receive an energetic boost of Universal proportions
translating into super-charged support for current endeavors

Sandy Grason has this to share on recording Gratitude:

"When you slow down long enough to notice the details
around you
you will be awed by the beauty and abundance in the world.
This is a good time to
express your thankfulness for all that you have and all that
you are going to create
in your life. Keeping a Gratitude journal is nothing more
than writing down a few things
each day that you are grateful for, yet this practice holds
magical powers – you will begin to look for things
throughout your day to write down . . .once you get going,
Gratitude will over flow from your journal because there
are so many things to be grateful for.

Therein lies the magic of expressing Gratitude in your journal.
It connects you to a state of appreciation that
spills over into everything you do and experience. It inspires
you to view your life through a state of grace –"

'Journalution –journaling to awaken your inner voice, heal
your life, and manifest your dreams' by
~ Sandy Grason

The pen gains ground! The pen gains ground! It is Now
mightier than the sword!!!Aaahhhhhhhhhhh – at last.
Imagine – all this through one simple stroke of
Gratitude.

A few years ago, my Reiki Master (I am now one) suggested
the most powerful life changing practice – a gratitude journal!

It is praying for what you want/need/desire – as though you have already received it. IT is also expressing gratitude for WHAT IS.

I began, not knowing what to expect. I am a Rosicrucian and practicing mystic, so I believe in the unseen and powerful mind and heart. Yet, this was a venture into new territory . . . writing . . . expressing . . . acknowledging . . . accepting . . . believing . . .

I cannot begin to tell you the miracles that have occurred in my life and business as a result of this practice – blessing upon blessing – ask and you shall receive is true – not always as we envisioned, but true. But, more importantly, I can't begin to tell you the change it has wrought within me.

That is what convinced me to share in your gratitude vision and the 42 days of sharing and acknowledging gratitude.

Thank you for sharing your story and your vision. I thought I would share mine.

I KNOW that gratitude is one of the two moving forces of the universe – it is the other side of love – receiving and returning. Gratitude is the expression of our understanding of this blessing called life and the love of God. Without it, we are merely children – accepting the gifts of the universe without thought – gratitude makes us spiritual adults and co-creators of reality with God.

With love and gratitude
~ Brenda D.

CODED FOR CREATION
LESSON 14

Note
Divine Coding
contained within Gratitude:

egg = beginning = creation
spiral = journey = discovery
circle = completion = return to Now

This formula,
held sacred for all creative purposes,
Will Divinely structure Now
to
support
all generations Living in Love.

Go Gratitude!

One coded key to living mastery, unlimited creative license
and Divine Will – You are soooooo prepared.

A Sacred Geometry Experience

Introduction :

Sacred Geometry is the blueprint of Creation and the genesis
of all form. It is an ancient science that explores
and explains the energy patterns that create and unify all
things and reveals the precise way that the energy of
Creation organizes itself.
On every scale, every natural pattern of growth or movement
conforms inevitably to one or more geometric shapes. As you
enter the world
of Sacred Geometry you begin to see as never before the
wonderfully patterned beauty of Creation.
The molecules of our DNA, the cornea of our eye,
snow flakes, pine cones, flower petals, diamond crystals, the
branching of trees, a nautilus shell, the star we spin around,
the galaxy we spiral within, the air we breathe, and all life
forms as we know them emerge out of timeless geometric
codes.
Viewing and contemplating these codes allow us to gaze
directly at the lines on the face of deep wisdom and offers up
aglimpse into the inner workings of the
Universal Mind and the Universe itself.
The ancients believed that the experience of
Sacred Geometry was essential to the education of the soul.
They knew that these patterns
and codes were symbolic of our own inner realm and the
subtle structure of awareness.
To them the 'sacred' had particular significance involving
consciousness and the profound
mystery of awareness –
the ultimate sacred wonder. Sacred Geometry takes on
another whole level of significance when

grounded in the experience of self-awareness.
~ lightSOURCE

. . . Imagine my surprise when I was opening my new clock for Christmas, a beautiful Zen timepiece that my daughter got me and the instructions included a lesson on the Golden Ratios. The beautiful bell will now awaken me at the rhythm of the Golden ratio. During a ten minute interval I will hear these resonant strikes at a progression that mimics the Golden Ratio. Unfamiliar with the ratio, I read on to find that the ratio represents beauty in the human body, the galaxy, everywhere in nature. The pamphlet goes on to explain that one of the most beautiful examples is seen in the nautilus shell or, "even on the side of your own fist." I quickly made a fist and looked at the side of my hand and saw the go gratitude sign. Wow! God has a sense of humor. Beauty and Gratitude are one in the same. Thank you.
~ Amy

GO
LESSON 15

Spell GO in one motion –
notice GO in Gratitude, a 'g' in front of a BIG 'O'.

Go Gratitude!

A direct connection exists between the big O in Gratitude's GO
and finding one's G spot. It is simply a matter of skill and
interest.
No less, know more!

more ... More ... MORE ...

To go into a space of creation simply flow through Love
to Gratitude. Imagine Gratitude, spinning through your
heart,
drawing in and pulsing out the energy of creation,
beat by beat, minute by minute, flowing through you
as a wave, meeting both your head and feet simultaneously.
Now feel this energetic flow returning to source, only to
be quickened once more by the spirit of life, each beat building

upon the last creating more, more, more Gratitude.

This place of creation, this heart center, this G-spot within the space of our human frame is our connection to divinity and our source of creation.

Simply know to Go and it is so.

Thank you Thank you Thank you. I have just completed my 42 days of Gratitude, and my whole world has altered. I have experienced the Source at work.

I invited into my life my Divine Lover. I gave thanks for him. I had not met him yet. Having spent 8 years since my last big relationship breakup I had grown resigned to a life alone.

Three weeks ago I said to the Universe, I invite him into my life, and Thank you. I drew a picture of him, a big heart with the words Thank You, surrounded by swirls of gratitude. That evening my neighbor came over and said 'Julia there is the most beautiful man at our house, you should come and meet him.'

I did. It was instant attraction for both of us. He walked me home, got my number, gave me a hug, called the next day. Three weeks later we are talking about moving in together. I thought you would like to hear, to add to your collection of miracles.

I am so grateful to everyone who crosses my path – for they all have something to teach me. Thank you for the gift of gratitude. Love and Thanks

~ Julia
(Melbourne, Australia)

LISTEN, LISTEN AGAIN, LISTEN DEEPLY
LESSON 16

Lay head to hands, supported by solid surface. Be still.
Listen. Listen again. Listen deeply.

Behold,
waking Gratitude
returning to Love YOU ~
every pulse flowing at heart's beat
greets a return wave,
bent back by guiding valves,
meeting each following generation of waking Life.

This meeting, this moment,
this standing wave of
past presently proving
a future moving Now
whispers,

'Listen –
all is well
all i swell
all i's well.'

Go Gratitude!

Play with your pulse ~ slowing, drawing and quickening the
beat.
listen as you Go to Gratitude.
listen again. now listen deeply.

Gratitude is shape and form, flowing as divine mirror of the
human ear.
check this out: G R A T I T U D E – an echo whispering
hidden truth's of Gratitude!
thanks, mom, for teaching me to listen, listen again, listen
deeply!

I am loving "Go Gratitude" I am having a big range of
experiences. I am an inventor and my inventions are taking on
a new life. Just prior to starting "Go Gratitude" I had a series of
inventions totally outside of my normal field of activity and they
are turning out to be major inventions that will go world wide
and be of major significance to many millions of people.

One invention is very significant to "Go Gratitude" it is a
new musical instrument based on the Australian Aboriginal
instrument called the "Didgeridoo" It is the shape of
"Go Gratitude" logo and I use it in conjunction with my
meditation using "Go Gratitude" and I enter a beautiful
state centered in the heart with a very steady integration
of physiology and spirit with a presence of love and inspiration.

The most remarkable thing has happened: I do volunteer work with aboriginal people and I was called to a meeting by them the other day and they said that even though I was not Aboriginal the elders all enjoy my company and respect the volunteer work I do and would I help them as an advisor on how to set up a new initiative to help create employment for Aboriginals as they have a new pool of government funding.

A week later I did a presentation to the elders about setting up a series of new patents in a company set up to bring benefits to all the aboriginal community. They are considering my proposal and will get back to me after Christmas. This new musical instrument is a part of the proposal, I have called it the Echo Stick because it doubles the intensity of the vibration and send the vibrations back down through your body as you play it.

The result is an increase in oxygen released to the cells of the body which has a major positive impact on your health. The vibrations are trance inducing (because they are received via auditory and vibrational receptors of the bone and ear simultaneously in the same way you received sound when you were in the womb) and this allows you to focus and intensify your will on what ever you choose to direct it to.

. . . This is a powerful therapeutic musical tool which works on increased oxygen reducing Disease symptoms) and increases the willpower, psychic and spiritual talents by harmonizing the vibrations of the body. If this is focused through divine inspiration it is a massively powerful tool.

~ Love Mike

UPSIDE OF GO (D)

LESSON 17

Look for divinity in simplicity
to find God in Gratitude.
~ hidden yet openly revealed ~
as One is willing to
knew-ly view
Go
as
God
Ok, luv.

What does simple Gratitude reveal
on the up-side of Go?

G – o
lift the veil, flip it over.

– d

of course! Go-d –
inverted as transparent spheres' mirror,
reflecting messages of Gratitude prove
believing IS seeing.

Go Gratitude!

As above, so below
So within, so without
Go Gratitude, so know God

"Gratitude arises when you accept the Wisdom of All That Is,
and that
the God Essence lives in All Things, no matter what
appearances may
be. Even times experienced as difficult, such as now, are
bridges to
Higher Levels of Consciousness, and so carry their own
blessings. Be
grateful that you may experience these deep changes that are
bringing great blessings to the Planet. The Love of the Source
moves
in All Things – even Now! And then, as you are able to feel
gratitude for All That Is, you will find Serenity and Peace. You
will feel a deep calm, and instead of fear and anxiety reactions,
you will begin to perceive the Great Mystery and Wonder at
the Heart
of the All. You will feel the Great Love in the Heart of the
Universe and you will know that All is Love, and that
everything in

your life is an expression of Love in some way. When you have allowed that recognition to open your Heart – then you will accept
the Gift of Joy. And will be able to transmit it to others. It is within you, in your deepest Heart, waiting to emerge and be expressed!"

~ Archangel Michael through Celia Fenn

I started with Go Gratitude and found out that the last message was on the day before my birthday. My birthday was in a way a new birth! Now being thankful, in Gratitude, is a way of living. Every day I thank people (and God) and 'all there is': without other people I do not exist, purely because they are me and they are a way for me to meet myself!

The symbol is already for years a special symbol for me . . . Now, what do I have to add—nothing—but : Thank you for sharing !!!!

~ Anja B

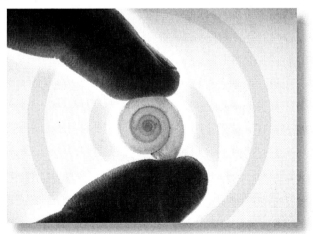

SIT AND SPIN
LESSON 18

Remember the toys —
round with a wheel centered
atop a turning post —
a disk to on which to
sit and spin.

A simple, youthful aid
to changing one's outlook on life.
Remember:

it IS just as easy
to shift Now by spinning into Gratitude —
feeling every pull, tug, churn and chug
along this turning ride.
Exciting, yes?

Go Gratitude!

BE
fountains of youth,
standing waves
whhirrrling, swirling to sur-face

shifting slightly –
just enough to
make wakes of Gratitude.
dizziness optional.

"The miracle of changed consciousness
comes from placing the attention
above the difficulties of the day.

With deep Gratitude
comes true humility,
a key to the Fountain of Youth.

Gratitude lights the way to enthusiasm.
Enthusiasm clears the path to Love.
Love is the key to freedom."
~ Sandy Paris

. . . I HAVE to mention to you that it was more than two and a half years ago that I had a very memorable dream about what you use as the gratitude symbol; the circle with the nine or six in it. I kid you not.

That particular dream was preceded by similar dreams earlier and in the years shortly before. The date was 1 August 2003 and I made a drawing of the symbol at that stage and added it to the notes of a book I am writing. I showed the drawing to my then housemate and still very good friend Anna-Marie. When your gratitude mailings and series started coming to me, I reminded my friend that this symbol was very very similar and almost the same as the three dimensional movement I had experienced and seen in my dream that eve. As you had explained in one of your Go Gratitude mailings and the way I understand it, the consciousness of benevolence could be spread through your intent of gratitude, and to balance awareness with starting a (k)new wave and turning it in to a 'see' (sea) of gratitude. Well, it certainly made a 'ripple' and entered my realm of energy as subconscious thought, and into my dreams . . .

As a result and matter of ascension and earth energy and consciousness rising, it just makes my natural evolution, re-membering and hobby as a healing healer so much more valid, easier/simpler, flowing and enjoyable! hehehehe and I can't help but giggle here 'coz it leaves me with a feeling of a child like "I told you so!" or rather, "I SOLD you so" when friends talk to me about their difficulties and I could help them through it with and from a loving perspective. . .

Regards and Namasté
~ Tiaan

ACROSTICLY TRUE TO GRATITUDE
LESSON 19

GROW.
REMEMBER.
ACCEPT.
TRADE.
INVOKE.
TREASURE.
UNDERSTAND.
DELIGHT.
EXPLORE.

Go Gratitude!

Hey! you can play, too.
Ready? GO.
Spell it out now ...
or perhaps you wish to take time
to consider a perfect arrangement for Gratitude.
In every event ~
just do it.

---

an excerpt:

(see photo for reference)

"while spelling ourselves into GRATITUDE
many questions popped up,
revealing simple instructions to be
insufficient for such a grande undertaking.

Q: how big shall I make my letter?
A: belly button to chin –   then our
    efforts are centered in the Heart.

Q: whose view are we using,
    ours or the cameras?
A: draw so others will know
    Gratitude when they see it.

Q: capitals or lower case?
A: let's capitalize on Gratitude –"

. . . My experience took place several years ago, as a recovering
alcoholic, I found myself very depressed and when I heard the
topic of gratitude – I became negative and annoyed, even angered
at those that found it to be a solution. Phrases like "Attitude of
Gratitude" literally annoyed me.

Yet one day, I had about 20 minutes to have to wait and was
terribly depressed and hurt due to a recent relationship breakup.
I found – out of desperation – to take pen and paper and began a

gratitude list. I started with the letter 'A' and decided that I could take my life afterwards, but first I would try to complete the list. I started with Air, Alex (my son) then to 'B' I was grateful for the Blues (good music) 'C' for my creativity as a musician, and so on. The harder the letter in the alphabet was, the more I had to think. The more I thought about gratitude, the more my brain was changing. It became an exercise.

I'd take a bike ride or walk and instead of being angry or worrying or resentful – I'd do the Gratitude Alphabet. Stuck in traffic or couldn't sleep – I'd do this exercise. I believe that this began a powerful change in my brain's chemistry and - 9 years later – has had amazing results. But the results were almost immediate. Just like the experiment with water, I began to change and attract good things and people in my life.

~ Dennis

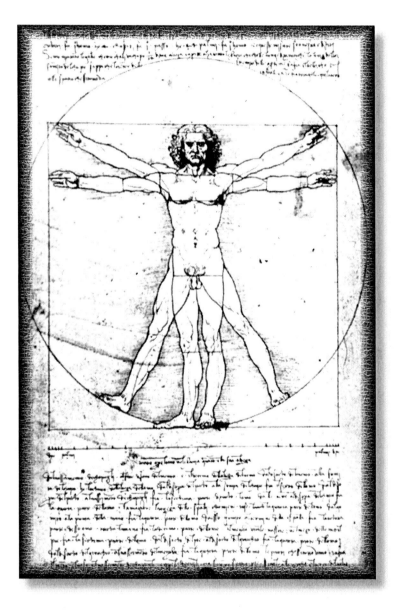

PRACTICE MASTERY IN GRATITUDE
LESSON 20

Practice is the art of learning
Mastery is the art of living
Gratitude is the art of Loving.

Go Gratitude!

By daily endeavor one discovers life is
simply an adventure in levels of Self.
Imagine mastering Now.
Wow.

———

"– a basic law:
the more you practice the art of thankfulness,
the more you have to be thankful for.
This, of course, is a fact.
Thankfulness does tend to reproduce in kind.
The attitude of gratitude revitalizes the entire mental
process
by activating all other attitudes, thus stimulating
creativity."

(Norman Vincent Peale,
—American pastor, Author 1898–1993)

I want to thank you personally for including me in this glorious wave of gratitude. For a long time I didn't believe I had much to be grateful about. After I became disabled, I would sit and watch the minutes of my life tick by and feel sad and sorry for my own loss.

I have a balance disorder which slowly worsened from the time I fell on the ice and hit my head at age 12. At age 36, my balance became so bad that I kept walking into walls and falling down and dropping things. Surgery on my ears to correct the problem only made things worse. The damage was such that I would have ended up using a walker and wheelchair eventually – the surgery simply hastened the inevitable.

I had been an R.N. I loved making a difference in people's lives. As a giver of solace and care, I had found my calling in this life and I loved it. Then it was all ripped from me and I was left spinning in misery. For a time, I couldn't even read or write because my co-ordination was so poor. I couldn't listen to music any more because I am deaf now. I felt I couldn't bear the loss of so much. All I did was sit and ask, "Why?"

Then my kids bought some clay and I started fiddling around with it. I made the most beautiful woman sitting on a rock reading a book. I had no idea I had this talent at all until so much had been taken from me. Working with the clay helped me regain some control over my vision and eye-hand co-ordination. But it was your Go Gratitude idea rolling around the planet that made me realize I could actually see this horrid damage in my balance system as something to be grateful for. If it had not happened, I never would have discovered my artistic talent. Nor would I have had the time to take advantage of it.

I am now incorporating the Go Gratitude symbol somewhere in every sculpture and painting that I create. I am teaching it to the children I tutor and to my granddaughter. Every day we find things to be grateful about together. See? There's something else! Unless I was disabled, I wouldn't have this time with her, either.

The reason I'm writing? Just a few moments ago I was staring at the large Go Gratitude symbol you sent out with the valentine. I closed my eyes and saw the image of the symbol still remaining. But the symbol didn't fade like images do normally. It kept getting brighter and pulsing. And it turned back to green.

And, at about the 11:00 area, a kind face appeared for a moment. And then – wings! All over the place!! It was amazing!!!

I'm not one to buy into the opiate for the masses, but I can't deny being a spirit having a physical experience. I simply wanted to share this with you so you would know how deeply the wave of gratitude has touched me.

Many thanks,
~ Sue Ann

HOW TO CREATE (INSERT CHOICE HERE).

LESSON 21

Remember a moment
of true Gratitude.

Now
breathe deeply
this powerful memory,
a charge of energetic elixirs
delivering perfectly mixed messages
to fully appreciate this past moment
of You.

So it is to Create, as well.

Simply remember Gratitude to
draw this creative elixir by Will,
as it flows on notice
and command.

Remember to structure activities
in order to prepare
to artfully receive all you conceive.

Breathe deeply once more – exhale pure essence of Now to
acknowledge, accept, and appreciate knowing

You know Gratitude.

Go Gratitude!

It sounds so simple, and yet – it IS!
Let's put it this way:
1. Gratitude   2. Will   3. Deliver

"The more gratefully we fix our minds on the Supreme
when good things come to us, the more good things we
will receive, and the more rapidly they will come;
and the reason simply is that the mental attitude of
Gratitude
draws the mind into closer touch with the source
from which the blessings come. If it is a new thought
to you that Gratitude brings your whole mind
into closer harmony with the creative energies of the
universe,
consider it well, and you will see that it is true.
The good things you already have come to you
along the line of obedience to certain laws.
Gratitude will lead your mind out along the ways by
which things come; and it will keep you in close harmony
with creative thought and prevent you from falling
into competitive thought."

~The Science of Getting Rich by Wallace D. Wattles

Here's a story – My Mother who is 88 years old finally sold the family home that I grew up in with my 5 brothers and sisters for 48 years (I'm 54).

She moved out of the house in July and we cleaned everything, everything out the house for her move. We cleaned out closets, nooks, crannies, everything was cleaned out. So she moved in July and in January I found myself driving in the old neighborhood just to see the old house I grew up in and I noticed the new family had not moved in yet, but were doing some major construction with new wiring and such.

As I drove down the street I saw a workman hop out of an electrician's truck and was walking on the sidewalk to go into the house. I pulled up in my car next to him, stopped where he was and asked if he was working in the house, he said "Yes". I paused and said "You know, I grew up in this house." He was interested in knowing that so he invited me to come see some of the new construction.

I walked with him and look around as he guided me through some newly created spaces. I was showing him the second floor bedroom I shared with my two sisters and noticed the ceiling was opened up to the attic so that he could communicate with the electricians doing the wiring up there. He yelled up to the workers, introducing me as "this lady who grew up in this house." One of the workers in the attic hesitated and then said "You know, I found a picture of a lady up here in the attic – do you want to see it?" I told him 'Yes' so it took a few minutes for him to bring down the attic stairs with this very dusty package of photos in an old photograph box.

He handed it to me. I recognized the box immediately and opened it up. I was amazed to see the portrait of my 17 year old self. Included were a portrait of my 4 year old self, and my 10 year old self. Portraits of me that had been left behind in my childhood home for whatever reason.

I had to recognize my finding and reclaiming of myself at this time in my life as a miracle. Really a miracle of gratitude and want to share that once embarking on a path of gratitude our lives can go full circle, of reclamation, acknowledgement, affirmation, exploration and anticipation for what other miracles are to come.

I'm excited to see what's next – just as excited to see the next message on gratitude. Thank you for your work. It is pivotal in people's lives, has been for me!

~ Anonymous

WHIRRLED PEACE

LESSON 22

I am centered in Gratitude
as a hurricane gathering rain

peaceful
to be at the
heart of Now.

Imagine –
our shower of waking whirrled peace
Will flow through Now
easing thirst
clearing space
activating abundant seeds
gathered
as blessings of time.

Go Gratitude!

As order to chaos
one witnesses' change.
Remember –

even
Gratitude
lives through hurricanes.

Each situation in your life exists for your spiritual growth and
evolution and when you are ready to acknowledge the wisdom
with which you organize the scenarios of your life, you will
learn to love each situation. Then you can become aware of its
lessons, know and learn them and love them free.
Once you learn to love the experience, it has fulfilled its
mission in your life and can depart from you. But as long as
you continue to hate, judge, resent, run away from or ignore
it, it will exist and even intensify as it mirrors everything you
dislike about it. Is it good or bad, right or wrong, beneficial or
harmful, short term or permanent – all of these are judgments
that will only result in the continuation of the circumstance.
Instead, ask your Self, 'what do I need to learn from this'
and you will take the first step on the path to freedom Each
difficult experience that you have is a mirror of a fear in your
life – discover the fear and the reason for its existence and
it has no power over you and then ceases to exist unless you
allow it to. The more dire the situation, the greater your need
to learn and appreciate its lesson and heal
that aspect of your belief system.
Once you acknowledge that you created the reality, it loses
its power because it is the paradigm that you built, not the
result of someone else's actions against you. Then you can
love it free and move on to create other realities that are
more peaceful, joyful and fulfilling. No matter what the
circumstance, if you can learn to love it,
you can free yourself from it

and move forward on your journey.
~ Archangel Uriel through Jennifer Hoffman

It has been quite a journey and I thank you deeply from my heart and mind and soul, and whole being Sometimes flashing moments of inspiration . . . soul   direction . . . illumined thought . . . emotional calmness . . . heartful thanks . . .

. . . Sometimes chaos, bringing up those dark and unloved places to be renewed and brightened by the group love and light and guidance. They have all been gifts leading us forward.

The reminder of gratitude each day has led me to be more grateful for life itself, more compassionate for myself leading to a greater loving understanding and compassion for others. It also has lightened and brightened my days, reminding to play and enjoy. Life and all we have are gifts to be enjoyed and shared. I have also realized that wherever we are at this time is perfect for us and trust is growing in my being.

With much love and gratitude,
~ Kate

STAIR WAY TO HEAVEN
LESSON 23

Imagine Gratitude spinning
~ centered on axis ~
by 90 degrees each turn

Opening,
by entropy's call,
a way to reach any chosen space –
to give lift to any focused charge, intention, and command –

an on-demand
stair way to heaven.

Go Gratitude!

90 degree turns may also re-present
earth's four directions, a cross, and
humanity's four appendages.
Turn to Gratitude in times of intentional living,
rising to meet each challenge as Gratitude

lifts US to heavenly heights of earthly ecstasy.

Notice the 9-0 in Gratitude ~
merely a turn of perspective, yes?

"Let me emphasize here that while Gratitude is
the keystone, it's desire that gets the arch started.
Without desire, entropy would end all life.
The desire for 'more better' is embedded in life,
driving innovation and transformation.
Gratitude is the keystone in the arch of prosperity.
To the person who knows nothing of the construction of
arches, they could appear to be held up by 'invisible means of
support.' Likewise, someone who knows the process of making
arches need not understand how it all works to construct a
functioning arch.
By making gratitude the center of my relationship with the
universe, I am placing the keystone where it belongs. And like
an arch, I too have invisible means of support"
~ the Milieu

. . . I must share what is in my heart. For some time I have
practiced the law of Gratitude. I absolutely know that it is a true
principle and it works for creating healing, abundance, peace
and joy, to name only a few. I AM Grateful for the beautiful tools
(you) are providing.

They come in very handy now as I am in the process of
supporting my new husband through a healing crisis. He has
experienced some very difficult years and is now opening his heart
to love and light, more than at any time in his entire life. We are

learning together that the Gratitude that we feel in the simple act of finding one another is a positive force that literally transforms anything that is not of the light.

Miracles are daily occurrences in our life and we acknowledge them as such. No, life has not stopped placing lessons in our path, but we embrace them with Gratitude even as we once would have whined and complained about them.

Yours in Gratitude,
~ Susan E.

THE ART OF GRATITUDE
LESSON 24

Follow three rules to artfully create a masterpiece of
Gratitude:
1. All shapes are self contained. Beginning to End
Seamless.
2. Space exists between all Shapes.
3. Go with the Flow.

Go Gratitude!

The art of Gratitude is respecting natures laws to
create inspired time with flow and ease.
In one motion, Gratitude honors all three rules above
Amazing.

"The essence of all beautiful art, all great art, is Gratitude"
~ Nietzsche

Included is a personal piece of "Gratitude Art."

Upon closer examination you will discover space between each completed shape, whether simple or intricate.

My secret?
Go with the flow of Now and let the message emerge.
Enjoy!

As you feel inspired, take a few moments to create a masterpiece of your own!
Be centered in Gratitude and remember -
1. Shape   2. Space   3. Flow – now GO!

I began drawing on the paint program on my computer, free flowing gratitude symbols and played with colors and ended up with . . . negative space images. I like to think of filling negative space with gratitude as creation from the void, and reaching from within to move out. "Split a piece of wood, I am there. Lift a stone, I am there." from the scrolls supposed to be Jesus' own writing. The kingdom of heaven is within each of us.

Blessings,
~ Christi

A PATH OF GRATITUDE
LESSON 25

Follow a path of Gratitude to loosen
neck and shoulder muscles.

Begin by dropping shoulders to rest lightly below
your ears. Now gently allow the head to follow gravity's pull,
falling to curve round, forming a center of gratitude.

Continue to release stored tension
by flowing slowly, deeper into the spin
ear drawing near the shoulder
making a complete journey to meet
full circle
while mindfully stretching
Body to Soul
Spirit to Source
Self to Now

In order to honor balance
bend your brain round this:

Reverse this exercise to draw a mirror
image of Gratitude activating Alpha and Omage within.
Repeat 'til you feel complete.

Go Gratitude!

"You must approach your yoga practice with reverence and
gratitude and love.
It's very much like entering a temple."
~ Amrit Desai

A loose neck allows greater mobility for
glimpsing present opportunities.
Using Gratitude as a pattern Will align Self
to notice, follow, and enjoy Divine promptings.

For your consideration:

What opportunities may be just out of view,
accessible by stretching your mind-body-spirit-essence
through an exercise in Gratitude?

As I read through each day, wonderful things are happening
all around me. First almost unnoticed little things started to
happen, when I started to look at my life as wonderful as it is, so
special.

I am learning so many beautiful things about my life, and
gratitude. It really does begin there. The more I consider this in
everything, the more I see!! It's simply amazing!!

The feelings of Love, and forgiveness surround me all day now.

Every moment is filled with someone bringing me a message of love and wisdom. As I create my new life, with gratitude first, everything has changed for me.

I know this is probably not the best reply you have received to date, but my intension was to tell you how grateful I am that I "stumbled" across this 42 of gratitude.

You have helped me understand so much about myself, my life, and caring for others.

Thank you so much!! You have no idea how you have helped this humble shepherd realize his beautiful life that was made with him in mind!

Love,
~ Daniel

THEARTOFGRATITUDE
LESSON 26

the art of Gratitude

+he art of Gratitude

+ heart of Gratitude

IS

YOU

Go Gratitude!

Through time, translation and change
meanings will be rearranged -
simply seek to be heartfully centered in
Gratitude and all possibilities will be revealed to YOU.

Neale Donald Walsch in the
'Conversations With God' series
artfully displays various ways

to change old views into new knews.
remember = re-member
intimacy = into-me-see

re-member too real-eyes what's happyning NOW as YOU Be
Come Gratitude!

----------◆----------

'Just meditated on the G symbol.' I think I need to tell you
what came . . .

I sat first and brought in the white light, then asked for my
guides to be present. I gazed at the G symbol and began in my
mind to give thanks for my life, going through all the things that I
am grateful for, the safe welfare of my children, the improvement
in my health after 4 years of illness, the roof over my head, food
on the table, my abundance of good friends and so on. I found I
was drifting off and could see not one but 2 G symbols. 1 had a
black centre and 1 had a white centre similar to Yin and Yan.

I then perceived a light stream emitting from my heart, it
connected to another light, which in turn connected to another
light and so on. This continued until there was an enormous
web looking blanket of light, all connected and resembling DNA
strands. Then into my mind came the earth or the world, a sphere
in space. I could see to the centre of the earth, there was a huge
fire, growing larger and larger like a volcano about to erupt. I saw
the earth vibrating.

This was quite scary. Then floating along was this huge web
of our light, enormous, so enormous it wrapped itself around
the earth and instantly the vibrations ceased. I sat quietly in
meditation waiting for a personal message, not realising the

magnitude of what I had been shown. The next mind pictures were of different places in the world, lots of sunshine, and people with happy countenances. No fear, anger or hatred was showing on their faces. Then I heard my guide say, do you see it now. I must admit I am a bit slow at getting the message.

Anyway, my interpretation of this now – The gratitude that is being shown by all people involved in Go Gratitude is enough combined energy to calm the earth's troubled heart and bring peace to its inhabitants. It means much more, but I am not very good at putting words on paper, I do better talking about it. I think my head goes quicker than my fingers. Must say this is a very powerful program and I am delighted to be a part of it.

Blessings
~ Val M.

SPACE TO CHOOSE
LESSON 27

Gratitude creates space to
wholly-holy-holey
perceive Choice
as it swirls in levels of Self
offering knew views of whirrleds within worlds.

Beyond Self is Present Matters,
happynings near you offering you-know-what.

Using Gratitude
to guide encounters of Choice
Will   easily allow One to be perfectly positioned for
accepting returning blessings
and
unexpected treasures.

Go Gratitude!

Imagine Gratitude as periscope, portal, and peep hole –
allowing you to immediately
focus, magnify, explore
and perceive Now.

Choose-a-way!

"It is only by honoring your own creational being that you honor all that is holy, all that is divine and all that is earth. Do not wait, hoping someone will give you what your heart seeks – Give yourself what others in your life have not been able to give you. Do not shun them for not bringing you the gifts. The gift you give is the gift to yourself, of yourself, for yourself, and by yourself.

That gift is the remembrance that you are holy and born from the heavens – Through honoring yourself you enter into the Christ heart within your being and you will then rise to the next level of your light. But it is only through honoring your own divinity that you will be able to access this portal.
The portal of the Christ awaits you within.
Will you enter ?"

(Sananda through Gillian Macbeth-Louthan)

http://www.thequantumawakening.com

A few months before I joined the wave of Go Gratitude, another friend suggested I practice a simple technique for increasing my gratitude and sense of connection to the Divine Creatress by touching the earth once a day and thanking Her for my Life and All the wonder and abundance with which She blesses me. That was about 3 months ago.

I just returned from a 5-day trip where I got a job I wanted, a check to cover my moving expenses, found a great house to relocate to and had an incredible weekend on Sacred Land. Every moment was magical, full of a sense of community with unified intention, laughter, confirmation and an astounding flow of blessings and healing. This is a 180-degree change in the experiences of my life previously.

I thought you would be interested to know how Gratitude, in the many forms it is spreading, has been a miracle in my life. Keep the wave going . . . I'll be doing it on my end, too.

Namaste,
~ Brooke M.

BEYOND EGO
LESSON 28

Move beyond ego
by simply flipping to Gratitude.
Like this, for instance:

e –

insert arrow downward here!

– go

flip side of ego is Gratitude or – GO!

as a sentry keeping watch to give notice
of change, Ego covers our backside.

always present by design

~ on the Other side of Now ~

simply discipline Self
to focus on Go.

How?
ask ego anything –
in Gratitude.

Go Gratitude!

You will receive answers. Be prepared to accept what is given.
Daily engage with Self and re-member, too,
Listen. . . Listen again. . . Listen deeply.
Questions, of course, will elicit true response. Ask well

"So, the path of the co-creator is to be awakened spiritually
within, which then turns into your own deeper life purpose,
which then makes you want to reach out and touch others in
a way that expresses self and really evolves our communities
and our world. Certainly, we can't do that unless we activate
ourselves first. That's why, for me, emergence is the shift from
ego to essence That is so important."
~ Barbara Marx Hubbard

Circumstances have placed me in a temporary position in a family-owned company where the CEO is 26 . . . Everyone has amassed great wealth yet they don't seem to be working very hard, and no one is stressed.

I have found it profoundly irritating as I'm older and more experienced, and work very hard, though I've been struggling financially in my own business lately – it doesn't seem fair!

I've also known that I've landed in this situation to learn something from this family, and you've helped me identify it – the word is "resistance", and they seemingly have none, while I have a lot sometimes! Instead of standing apart I'm going to see what I can do to match their vibe. Thanks for the clue this morning!

I am grateful.
~ Bonny

DELIVERANCE
LESSON 29

Think outside the box.

Where to go?
Go to Gratitude.

Circular, transparent, open to interpretation.

In short, forget limits.

Allow universal deliverance
to appear
as uniquely designed
to meet current timing
by opening portals of possibility.

Go Gratitude!

"The box" indicates boundaries, limits, blind corners.
Just glance at Gratitude ~   graceful, open, go , Go, GO!
Deliverance, indeed.

Gratitude unlocks the fullness of life.
It turns what we have into enough, and
more. It turns denial into acceptance, chaos
to order, confusion to clarity. It can turn
a meal into a feast, a house into a home,
a stranger into a friend. Gratitude makes
sense of our past, brings peace for today,
and creates a vision for tomorrow.
~ Melody Beattie

I feel that gratitude came to me as my own natural evolution.
After years of wondering why certain things were not present in
my life, suddenly I realized I had so much to be grateful for.

It must be the same for everyone – all things arrive into the
consciousness at the right time. Other sources can inform you
and make you aware, but it is only when you are ready, that it
makes an impact.

Once I started to feel grateful, all my needs were met and now
I know I will always have enough and I will always be taken care
of. At about the same time I started to 'surrender' all my worries
all my fears. So gratitude and surrender have transformed my
life.

Love and gratitude
~ Barbara E.

SEED MAKER
LESSON 30

Imagine Gratitude
as a knew~ly planted seed of wisdom,
created wholly by choice.
Tenderly remember
to seasonally adjust sowing of seeds
in order to
lovingly manage space
for waking realities
to grow
naturally.

Remember –
old, un-intentioned, rotten seeds
will waste away
returnin
to
Source
as matter in time
to nourish
Now.

Let these Go – focus is energetic flow.

BE current.

Go Gratitude!

Plant wildly with passionate pursuit.
All Will gather, as imagined.

Sow a thought and you reap an act; Sow an act and you reap a
habit; Sow a habit and you reap a character; Sow a character
and you reap a destiny.
— Samuel Smiles

. . . Deep within people's souls, you are planting seeds and
removing "weeds". Your authenticity and integrity shine through
with every word you write.

I am so grateful to have been sent Go GRATITUDE. It has
changed my life in so many ways and really has been the missing
link all along. I am a deep, passionate, compassionate and
loving person but for so many years now I have had this
intense unexplainable sadness and loneliness. I now realize that
it is all about gratitude. I was focusing on what I didn't have as
opposed to what I did (do) have. The most amazing realizations,
connections, awakenings etc have been manifesting ever since I
started reading GO GRATITUDE.

. . . Again, I cannot begin to explain how much I resonate with
your thoughts and beliefs. I am on "the same page" with both you
and your partner and think it is so amazing what you are doing

for people. You are literally changing the world by helping people to realize that truly helping is not about giving and making people co-dependent but rather inspiring people to find and live their own truth and to stand in their own power and to live a self-actualized life. In turn, by living and sharing our own unique soul prints, we are allowing people to do the same--there is no better feeling than accepting ourselves and having the freedom to be who we really are. This truly is the best gift ever and I am so thankful to you, Stacey for coming into my life to re-inFORCE this.

. . . Thank you so much for what you are doing. I am truly inspired. I love the way our world is heading--towards peace and love. It is people like you who are making this dream a reality.

Respectfully,
~ Lesley S.

WHOLE NOTE
LESSON 31

Egg-ly shaped,

centered on vibrations line,

is a note held whole.

Supported by time as symbol of Go,

flowing vibrations creating

scores of living Light.

Musically inclined by nature,

use whole note as an indicator,

timing gaps to accent Now –

– lingering long to center Self

by

quickening linear arrangements

with flair, style, and grace!

Gratitude supports notes by turns

of agreement with natural law,

symbolizing inner support of outer presence.

note worthy, indeed.

Go Gratitude!

muse-i-call-ye – how does Gratitude sound to You?

Aqua Vitae Quabbalisticae :

'In this step, the elemental power of each letter
is enlivened through feeling.'

'Each letter is pronounced as a color in any shape

that inner guidance directs, and is also toned to a musical note

that enlivens the color on an emotional level if toned inwardly,
and in the physical if toned out loud.'

G-R-A-T-I-T-U-D-E

'G, emerald green, Grace and Mercy, is subject to the
water principle of feeling and the exercises have to
be combined with a feeling of chill, which has to be increased
to a feeling of iciness.' [musical note F]

Letter R, golden, inner guidance, is subject to the earth
principle and the feeling of weight.' [musical note C]

'umlaut "A" , transformation and the mysteries of life and
death – he must have the feeling of a leaden weight, and stand
it through. He must be able to extend the feeling of weight to
the whole universe, and vice versa,
pass through this feeling of weight, represented and effected
by letter umlaut "A: from its expansion over the whole
universe down to a very small dot.[musical note C]

'Letter T, dark brown, high inspiration, appertaining to the
fire principle, too, is connected with a feeling of warmth.'
[musical note F]

'Letter I, light opalescent, cause and effect, is a letter of the
earth element and must therefore be practiced with a feeling
of weight.' [musical note G]

'Letter T, dark brown, high inspiration, appertaining to the
fire principle, too, is connected with a feeling of warmth.'
[musical note F]

'The U, velvet black, the act of creation and its ongoing effects, is analogous to the pure akasha principle and, when practiced, is connected with a feeling of penetrating everything.' [musical note B]

'Letter D, dark blue, the mysteries of love in creation, is controlled by the pure element of fire, or will, thus the quabbalist must have a feeling of warmth when he utters it. Depending on his ability of concentration and imagination, he must intensify this feeling up to a sensation of heat.' [musical note C]

'The deep purple E, omnipresence, has the specific characteristic of the akasha principle, of pure being and oneness with the Unified Field, which is revealed, in its elemental effect, in a feeling of power of penetrating all.' [musical note C]

notes of Gratitude:
F-C-C-F-G-F-B-C-C

enjoy this musical arrangement – you simply add meter, voice and feeling to sing your own song of Gratitude.

Information of the divine virtues and the letters
are referenced from
THE KEY TO THE TRUE QUABALLAH,
ISBN 3-921338-12-4].
Publisher is Dieter Rüggeberg, Wuppertal/W.

. . . I wish I had the language or the graphics to adequately lavish you with deserved multiplicities of exponentially outrageous Gratefulness –

Unfortunately, all I have is THANK YOU's, of every hue and pattern, of every note and chord, of every rhythm and cadence, echoing and blazoning and reverberating throughout my World and Universe . . .

Go Gratitude has changed my life incredibly – BLESSINGS BRIGHT AND BEAUTIFUL on You and Yours, and on ALL of us –

Wishing You Only WELL!

Huge Hugs and Love,
~ April and Ray

Go Gratitude!

BALANCE
LESSON 32

Give too Receive
Receive too Give
balancing Gratitude equally
in favor of collective
abundance.
Giving presents an opportunity to be open to all
sources for offering a justly-tailored trade.
Receiving allows us to gracefully conduct exchange
in order to accept what is presently offered
for mutual benefit.

Go Gratitude!

Blessed be to give and receive,
balancing Divine law of Reciprocity.
It's all circular, my luv.

"There is not a common denominator here, although
I must say, there was a shift when I deliberately
began to feel love, joy and Gratitude for the

ABUNDANCE I ALREADY HAD
in my life, which included the love of self, family and friends,
a safe and nice home to live in where I set my energies
of peace and harmony, a good job I enjoy (I work weekends
only) that is well paid and I have loving interaction with
everyone I meet – that enable(s) me to enjoy my perfect
health to continue my Spiritual work. I have personally found
that the ATTITUDE OF GRATITUDE works a powerful magic
energy and therefore I attract what I am giving out.
THANK YOU"

Love and light to you and yours,
~ Pam Lau

A couple of years ago I was in contact with a wise woman in
Australia who shared with me some beautiful words to remind
me that balance is so important. I would like to share them with
you because I have gained so much from reading and passing on
your words of wisdom and gift in sharing:

'I am free to give and receive with grace and ease
I am connected to the divine within'.

I felt my skin prickle all over with the strong connection
between yours and the words I received.

I have been guiding my own journey with the support and love
of some people in my life. With every message I receive from you
reinforces my thoughts and my journey. I thank you for that. I
have grown so much over the last couple of weeks and genuinely
believe that my growth and belief in myself is also influenced by
the beauty in your words. I thank you for that.

The combination of nature, creativity and yoga is bringing together in me an evolution that is truly great. I can see myself becoming one with myself. Instead of focusing on the negative of what people say and do I now see (mainly) the positive. Evolution takes time as the body's pattern changes and so does the perception of those around me. It is marvelous, fantastic, amazing, wonderful, exciting and most of all I am sharing it with many, not necessarily through the passing on of the emails but through me just being me.

I am so grateful that my friends gave me the opportunity to grow and move on.

Thank you.
My warmest hug and thanks,
~ Elise

SAY IT, SAY IT, SAY IT
LESSON 33

Pre-sent

present

Present

now say Gratitude after each one.

a simple shift of emphasis, tone, tense
-with added focus on Gratitude – will reveal (k)new
meanings Now.

Go Gratitude!

open sesame = open says me

"We can break the cycle – we can break the chain
We can start all over – in the new beginning –
We learn, we teach, We share
the myths, the dream, the prayer
The notion that we can do better
Change our lives and paths
Create a new world
and
Start all over
Start all over
Start all over
Start all over

We need to make new symbols
Make new signs
Make a new language
With these we'll define the world
and
Start all over
Start all over
Start all over
Start all over –"
~ Tracy Chapman,
'start all over',   New Beginning

I've known for many years that gratitude was a "Master Key" to reaching my purpose on the spinning blue marble we all call home. It has kept me on a path that keeps me from the "old ways" that drug me down to a level I would never have believed possible in my spent youth.

I have risen from behind a dumpster in a medium sized California city and now pass on a message of hope to other who are in the same sort of desperation I was in 15+ years ago. I write a gratitude list each night before retiring with at least 5 miracles in my life that I am thankful for.

... Your story has given me hope and joy and faith in my Higher Power . . . remember that it is the Universe's time that magic occurs. Thanks you again and I wish the greatest gift for you – love in peace.

~ John G.
Go Gratitude

SPIRALING IDEAS
LESSON 34

Energy flows in waves
following fractals to pattern order in chaos.

Ideas channel in this same manner,
prompting receiver to translate, record, organize, and share
inspired time.

At times, a vortex forms
~ too powerful for a physical body to orderly process ~
causing energetic outbursts, friction
and chaotic happynings.

By drawing Gratitude, a physical opening is created
for this abundance of energy to flow.

1. Grab a writing instrument.

2. Doodle gratitude

3. Continue to doodle thru Gratitude
'til a feeling of order presides.

Remember ~ follow this simple process
to direct creative energies thru physical channels
into viable endeavors.

Go Gratitude!

Over time you may be drawn to turn these therapeutic
exercises
into art, amassing a collection of intimate creativity born of
Gratitude.

On using spirals (Gratitude) to pass through
energetic blockages:
"That night, after seeing the attractor vortex in the water,
I was worried when I saw too many tics in the face of my son.
I suggested he make scrabbles and lines on a paper.
I said to him:
"Try to feel the energy that is inducing you to make
grimaces with your facial muscles."
He drew spirals at the same rhythm that he was moving
his lips, his eyebrows, and his nose.
He passed those energetic forces from his face to
his hand by drawing,
until he became conscious of the field that
was disturbing him.
My conclusion is that his tics were like an attractor, a spiral,
a pulsating vortex for his muscles;
they were like a probability wave that made him execute
Fixed Action Patterns- – FAP;
those tics disappeared when his hands and his gymnastics
absorbed
the energetic "spiral"
that before were expressed as tics (unconscious Gymnastics).

To draw lines and scrabbles on the paper was another
pulsating spiral that absorbed the force of his hand."

http://www.sensoterapia.com.co/qbits.htm

INTENTIONAL KARMA
LESSON 35

Circular thinking creates structures for
receiving abundant returns.

In order to receive stored blessings,
one must believe it possible, conceive a plan
and follow this journey to Source.
Full circle. Complete.

Imagine – creating 'then' Now by simply believing, conceiving
and receiving – all in the name of Gratitude!

Go Gratitude!

"Old school karma" got all twisted up
in an illusion of eternity.

nowhere to go? now here to Go.

twisted how simple it is –
write before hour eyes spelling space
into for-ever –

"Karma illustrates the circular energetic nature
of the universe. Energy doesn't move in a linear format,
but rather arcs back to itself as a vibration in an ever
widening, narrow and concentrated circle.
(editor's note: sounds like Gratitude)
Every energetic impulse that the self projects eventually
returns to the self, precisely the way it was issued out."

"Karma, a gift from the universe, provides a guideline for
the Soul's evolutionary curve. It is the road map through
which the self describes the specific journey of the Soul
in this particular lifetime. Ultimately fair, karma
establishes cosmic justice. The Law of Karma is EXACT –
Karmic Law dispenses the lessons which are uniquely
tailored to the individual student."
– KARMA' the Soul Connection By: Elizabeth Joyce

I have recently been working with the concept of Gratitude,
and your timely offering is a most direct reinforcement of the
knowledge that I am on the right track in wanting to clean up my
karma so that I can be a positive force for good in this world. So,
Thank You.

Much Love,
~ Roberta

SPELLING GRATITUDE
LESSON 36

Challenge: write Gratitude 100 times .
Hint: write ' Gratitude 100 times ' .
Challenge: spell Gratitude in one motion
Hint: draw above symbol

Gratitude is as complex as a Symbol
or as simple as remembering
to quickly think
outside the box.

Go Gratitude!

think this one thru: 9 letters or one – you choose.
time is of the essence.

get this:
the Word Gratitude has Nine Letters
Nine is a number of Completion
(note Nine in above Symbol)

our ability to express Gratitude has just taken a quantum leap,
joining all races, nations and tongues.
Now everyone can spell Gratitude easily!!!
write on –

About a week ago, I was sitting with my friend Brandi, and she began speaking in another language (tongues – she has done this before) and she prayed and prayed and cried and then looked at me. She put her hand on my forehead and she began sobbing and praying – then in English, she channeled a message. The last part of the message said "I have much GRATITUDE and Love for YOU."

It struck me – the use of the word "Gratitude". I have not forgotten that part of the message (or any other part) – but I have heard the word "gratitude" several times since then. Then today, I read this message and saw that symbol, and something inside of me clicked. I think this is collective consciousness again, at work! Amazing!

Love to you all,
~ Leanne

LIFE SAVER
LESSON 37

Imagine Gratitude as a ring
designed to
– buoy spirit, give lift, aid shift –
for rest on waking waters.

In event of turmoil and trial
simply send an S. O. S. call in order to

Serve Our Self
Sense Our Source
Support Our Soul

Re-member:
our SOS call may be altered
in honor of Gratitude
to reflect, empower, and support us

Now.

Go Gratitude!

To use Gratitude as life saving device,
simply remember to toss troubling thoughts
and center self – floating gracefully through rough waters to
peaceful shores –
giving thanks for ever more.
for sure, for shore.

Beliefs have the power to create and the power to destroy.
Human beings have the awesome ability to take any
experience of their lives and create a meaning that dis-
empowers them or one that can literally save their lives.

– Anthony Robbins

I read your . . . line about waking in the morning and instantly
it hit me that this is my pivotal time of day. I often wake with very
uneasy feelings, and sometimes have difficulty shaking them
throughout the day. It is recent that I have started waking and
consciously writing what I am thankful and grateful for knowing
for some reason this is an inner starting place of not only peace
but true success in life.

I am thankful today, grateful if you will, that we are all spirits
that come to feed each other. It is our ability to stay connected
that we provide each other with the ability to see a little more
than we would see on our own. Together we change the world.
Thank you for your work. We are ONE
Sincerely
With GRATITUDE
~ Mark C.

COMPASS-ION
LESSON 38

Imagine Gratitude as an ionic compass.
All ways present, always present, all ways Present.
Simple to grasp, easy to use.
Compassion ~ an ionic compass ~ will offer direction
as skillfully employed,
transparently utilizing intentional mastery
to direct our waking reality in
passionate pursuit of abundant
Peace, Love and Gratitude.

Compassion points out unique opportunities by
reading current streams of Waking Dreams,
directing attention to influential matters, while providing a
reference to gather a true sense of NOW.

Go Gratitude!

Guided to serve, many will thrive with Gratitude as a
Divine partner in compassionate communications.

Can you hear me now?

When we develop a right attitude of compassion and
gratitude,
we take a giant step towards solving our personal and
international problems.

~ H.H. Dalai Lama

To Stacey and the ground crew of Go Gratitude,
. . . Something . . . (a) Wave of Gratitude . . . has had a profound
effect on my life in the past 6 weeks. Slowly, over that time, I
have experienced a subtle but definite shift in my own attitude
and realize that 6 weeks ago I was not in a very positive place.
Now I find myself singing, being creative, and treating people
(with whom I had been upset) with much more compassion.
Thank you!

~Mary Lu

GIFT OF GRATITUDE
LESSON 39

Considering justly
time spent on giving gifts,
one is well to re-member this:

Think outside the box.

Use
Gratitude
to
heartfully choose
which gifts Will benefit whom.

Always and in all ways be prepared to share.

Go Gratitude!

Present Gratitude with intent, intuition, and insight
opening Now to Love.

> Feeling gratitude and not expressing it is like
> wrapping a present and not giving it.
> ~William Arthur Ward

Thank you . . . for sharing your knew views with us all . . . such marked shifts in my life since I signed on for this little experiment – Thank you!

In the last month and a half? I'm spiraling into my higher self, realizing my potential, manifesting the perfect people and situations to help me do so. My work and its opportunities for it (I'm a freelance writer) are vibrating. I've met an incredible fellow who feels like a kindred spirit. Old belief systems are dropping away. Everything is brightening and becoming more clear . . . and I believe it very much has to do with these daily . . . affirmations that you have planted . . . what a great gift!

I've sent this to a few of my friends and hope that they will take the time to make it happen for themselves, too. It's funny, in our hectic and busy lives, gifts like yours could easily be missed . . . I know I delete many messages without a blink. But I think the universe knew I was ready to receive your wisdom . . . Thank you!!!!

With love and light and of course, gratitude,
~ Cricket D.

PAID IN FULL
LESSON 40

As told,
current brain mass being accessed
is
ten percent.
That's it.

So, what's present in the other ninety percent?

Pure Gratitude.
By simply giving
ten percent in all matters
~ as attention, effort and tithe ~
You Will complete
circular appreciation
by simply offering a return of shared abundance.
Note figures below:
you @ 10 %

+

Gratitude @ 90% =

_____

100 % paid in full

Go Gratitude!

Nice set up. Neatly arranged. Simple to figure out.
Notice a nine before zero?

Now go –
tithe as inspired.

"Many people have had a psychological block against tithing
(giving), because so many theologians have stressed what
tithing would do for the church rather than what it could do
for the individual."
– Catherine Ponder, Open Your Mind to Prosperity

Cash is merely one gift we can tithe. Tithe with 10% of your work
time to volunteer activity. Tithe by giving 10% of journal time to
writing to those who are going through a difficult time. Tithe
by consciously giving full attention, listening without thinking
when speaking to anyone. Give 10% of your TV time: during the
commercials press MUTE and add to your list of gratitude for
what you have already. Gratitude energy feeds us and then we
can feed others . .

Love,
~ Cynthia

GO GRATITUDE
LESSON 41

In order to
create
flowing Grace
to
wrap time warp
as
Alpha Omega
space
Gratitude

IS

Now

GO

Go Gratitude!

Green means Go by collective agreement,
so relax –
it's all timed for a smooth ride.
Enjoy.

". . . Green is . . . unconditional love, inner healing and self-love. So now is the time to use Green energy to boost your love of self and assist you as you work to focus your mind in the direction you want to go. Bring some Green into your wardrobe and your home environment. Maybe a Green tablecloth would be great, or you could place some new Green plants on the porch this month? Put in a green bulb. Utilizing green energy will also help you to let go of your attachment to old behaviors, and help you to remember to give yourself a break as you work to create new behaviors and habits that will improve your ability to create the life you desire. Green will heal your heart and help you maintain a positive frame of mind."

http://www.wisdomcrystals.com/
crystalstaroraclebackissues.htm

I must thank you so much for sharing this blessed symbol. I have used it for healing by drawing the symbol over a photo of my beloved new grandson – we have healed his reflux in 24 hours and now mum and baby are both sleeping well and thriving, instead of the poor wee soul, projectile vomiting and crying non stop in pain thanks so much I will be using this symbol in a lot more energy work.

BRIGHT BLESSINGS
~ MAGGIE

WISHING WELL
LESSON 42

Imagine arriving at a
Universal Well of Gratitude,
to discover instructions for use.

Perhaps one might read this:

Well Come All.
This Source is pure, draw with pleasure.
Self reflection is highly encouraged, as calm
waters offer clear views. peer
deeply into watered wells – you may cast change
to invoke chance or chant charms for Love's romance.
Remember to heartfully pour forth all gathered
blessings so others will benefit, as well.

Go Gratitude!

Tossing change is one way to make waves.
Now be silent to hear whispers rippling from well tossed
offerings of Gratitude.

have you seen this?

WOW!

Carmen Colombo shares this on wishing:

Do you realize that if you Wish ONLY Well,
you can create your own world into what you wish?
And what is your own world?
It's the place in life where you are:
your present conditions, circumstances, family, friends,
work, environment – in other words, your LIFE.
By Wishing ONLY Well, you make your own world
AND
the whole world better.
It's neither altruistic nor selfish – it's logical!
You reap what you sow. Of course that doesn't mean that
exactly what you did will be done to you.
That would be too easy. It means that you will never know
the exact moment that you will shine or will fall,
depending on how you live your life.
Choose the high road, and expect the best.
You create your own world, and by extension the whole world,
every minute.

http://www.wowzone.com/wowintro.htm

· · · I realize I have had many changes, some that I would
normally have reacted quite negatively and strongly too but with
gratitude and love in my heart, I can genuinely thank the universe
and those involved for the opportunity to change or to learn.

I have quit smoking, without much drama or withdrawal and been grateful when I have had withdrawals, knowing that it is because I am working on giving up smoking, a desire I have had for many years.

I have made the decision to get out of my employment rut and look for work elsewhere while remaining grateful for and thus dedicated to the one I have.

I am undergoing a divorce and rather than being angry at or hurt by my ex as I have been, I am grateful for the lessons he teaches me and the reminder he gives me of the kindness of humanity, of my own humanity as well.

. . . I am so grateful for Go Gratitude and the constant reminders and opportunities to learn and apply that it offers. Funnily, or perhaps not, gratitude and forgiveness were two issues which I was confronted with a lot just before a friend sent this to me. She was not aware of my state of mind so it is not coincidental but synchronistic that she should send this to me. I am grateful to her too.

In love, I declare my gratitude to the universe, to all of humanity and to me and to YOU.

Thanks,
Martine B.

Go Gratitude!

CONGRATULATIONS!

You are a Master of Gratitude, embodying the key that opens all doors of possibility!

By the nature of your presence here, you are positioned to ride this world-wide wave of Gratitude. By being connected to a large group, consciously focused on using the divine tool of Gratitude, the powers of manifestation are amplified, a connection to the Creator within is present, and our collective consciousness is swimming in this source-force energy.

Simply amazing!

As you read this, a world-wide wave of Gratitude is flowing through hearts and minds across the globe. We are now forming the tides of change that will form the foundation for future generations to live a life of Love and Gratitude. Imagine the possibilities . . .

Now . . .

In honor of this Go Gratitude experiment, to appreciate what has passed, allow yourself to remember an experience, an idea, a single moment where you know Gratitude is making a difference in your life. As you tap into this pocket of time, connect each and every drop of water in your body to Gratitude as a living essence of Love. Let this memory flow gracefully through your body, giving thanks to YOU for making a conscious choice to heartfully connect to Gratitude.

As you go forward, use this connection to immediately return to the center of Gratitude, drawing on the power of your personal experience to propel current possibilities into waking reality!

Remember, as well, that each and every one of us will come to this moment having a vastly different experience, one uniquely suited to our personal journey yet universal in truth – **we are one in Love and Gratitude.**

Now, to answer a few questions . . .

To begin, you might wonder why we chose 42 as a number for the 'Knew views' series. You see, it takes 21 days to create a habit – this number is doubled to 42 in order to flow through to a level of Mastery.

As you choose to revisit memories of the past, you will surely discover instances where Gratitude is altering your current perception of your past experiences. Give thanks for this 'emotional alchemy'. As you Master Gratitude, you will naturally transmute leaden experiences into Golden moments.

Going forward, watch for Gratitude to appear at precisely the right moment to assist a shift or perhaps open previously hidden doors of possibility.

Additionally, each message in the '42 days of knew views on Gratitude' is designed to align the hemispheres of the mind by offering art with fact, idea with possibility and represents a balanced approach to life by following a structure called the Wheel of Transformation. This wheel consists of twelve unique arenas of Life arranged to create balance, wholeness and a multi-dimensional perspective

Each section is represented by at least three messages in the series, to further integrate Gratitude from a universal perspective with a wide variety of applications. Now, you may have noticed alternate spellings of certain words throughout the series. Are these typos? Absolutely! Intentional ones, of course.

Take (k)new for instance. You see, our spirits are connected to all things and it is simply our task to remember what time has forgotten. So new is really (k)new. Plus, it's a fabulous way to re-arrange old perceptions – a powerful tool during this time of Global transformation, to be sure. This is only one example of re-arranged spellings. You will likely discover many more as you begin to view the world through (k)new eyes.

Finally, this symbol of Gratitude is with you as a way to recognize ever-present truths; a great unifier emulated in every facet of life through art, nature, ancient civilizations and modern day revelations. Consider the symbol as a guide bringing recognition of what is present Now. In its highest form, **the symbol is YOU;** a living, loving Ambassador of Gratitude.

Remember – you are a Master of Gratitude.
You are the Key.

Now open all doors of possibility by creating a vision within your Heart, allowing your feelings to flow to your consciousness, creating a doorway for ideas, opportunities, people, and adventures to enter your life. Be grateful at every step, knowing that you are creating this experience and may choose to change course at any time.

As you are presently awakened to this power within, you are able to consciously create your daily experience. Being centered in Gratitude is empowering, enlightening, and ever so exciting!

Thank you for your presence on this amazing journey into the heart of Gratitude and for your belief that one person makes a difference.

That person is YOU!
Welcome to Now!

Go Gratitude!

NINE SUPER SECRETS FOR
SHIFTING INTO GRATITUDE

~ ONE ~
(K)new views on Gratitude

Gratitude opens all doors of possibility by creating multiple opportunities to view each choice, experience and moment anew. You see, by choosing to Go Gratitude, a multi-dimensional view is presented, allowing you to gracefully flow through Now to Joyful Well Being.

In order to creatively consider all possibilities, use this visual exploration to discipline the imaginative mind to lightly follow Love and Gratitude. Why lightly? Joy is aligned with Gratitude, present always and in all ways, to lightly present Now through You.

Use this exercise to discipline the creative mind to explore all possibilities by shifting into (k)new views on Gratitude:

Imagine Gratitude beginning to spin clockwise. Witness the speed increase as each turn becomes a blur to form a vortex. Listen for the roar of time churning to balance this state of change. Slowly spin Gratitude to a rest. Now spin Gratitude counter-clockwise, vividly witnessing with your minds eye a whirling, swirling state of Grace as you remember Gratitude will form a vortex both ways.

Now rotate Gratitude so you may view it from the side. Perhaps you will be surprised to see Gratitude is a spiral, stretching from tip through turns to bend round to Now.   In reality, a beginning and ending are merely illusions, created by a single point of view.   By imaginatively stretching one's perspective, (k)new worlds will open to you.

So it IS in all matters

Continue to cultivate creative visualization by spinning, flipping, stretching and bending Gratitude to your Will. Feel the colors, smell the sounds, taste the texture and hear the essence of this source force energy as you enhance present abilities to open (k)new doors of possibility by merely perceiving choice in change.

You will be cultivating a powerfully effective skill for clearly visualizing the life of your dreams.   As you energetically align with Gratitude you will find all signs are 'Go!' Go Gratitude!

~ TWO ~
Trance-Formation

As you become intimately aware of the presence, effect, and power of communicating with Gratitude, you will become aware of conversations where you feel resistance, that seem to be going nowhere . . . full of anger, judgment, fear or any number of other heavy emotions. In order to Trance-form any conversation into one flowing gracefully through Gratitude, consider using these three powerfully charming phrases:

1.   Perhaps ~
2.   Consider ~
3.   And Yet ~

Let's take a deeper look to view how each one will shift you into Gratitude:

Perhaps ~

Perhaps is a graceful way to keep opens all doors of possibility, by-passing a "yes/no" response while maintaining an opportunity to present an alternate point of view, a (k)new perspective or to further consider the moment at heart.

Consider ~

Consider is a gentle way to re-focus and direct attentions to (k)new opportunities, prompting rather than commanding a change in direction. Remember, rather than seeking to convince or convert you are simply offering a (k)new item for consideration. This cultivates feelings of choice, empowerment and respect, easily shifting Now into Gratitude.

And Yet ~

Using 'And Yet' easily allows possibilities to emerge, by opening an opportunity to present complimentary aspects of any topic . . . to highlight the lighter side of any topic or simply offer a change in perspective.

By weaving these three transition phrases into daily communications, you will discover it is a simple process to shift into Gratitude, trance-forming any conversation into a fluid meeting of heart and soul. Trance-form your words, shift into Gratitude and realize No where to Go is Now Here to Go. Go Gratitude!

~ THREE ~
EYE AM GRATITUDE

Stand in front of a mirror. Now relax, breathe deeply and remember a time when you felt the presence of Gratitude in your life. Allow this memory to flood through your body, re-connecting Now to this source force energy. As you feel immersed in this flowing wave of Gratitude, focus on the image before YOU and reflect the essence of this experience to your present Self.

As you project Gratitude to your reflection, imagine a beam streaming through your eyes, connecting your heart and the heart of the reflected image before you. Let this beam create a bridge, one that will carry your Love effortlessly between the inner you, and the one reflected by time.

As this bridge is now present, take a moment to look at your image. View what Gratitude looks like on you. Pay attention to how this feels – the arrangement of your facial muscles, your eyes, your breath, the peaceful countenance before you. Now give thanks to you for being YOU. As you feel Love and Gratitude infinitely reflected, close your eyes and re-create this image in your heart-mind. In vivid detail, allow your imagination to replicate the feeling, presentation, and essence of Love and Gratitude before you.

Slowly open your eyes, give thanks for NOW – and for the perfect being you are. Say to yourself: Eye AM Gratitude.

As you step away from the mirror, remember this: You, too, are a mirror of Gratitude.

By consciously projecting Gratitude to others – by essence, physical messages, and intent -you will instantly discover

Gratitude returning to you, reflected in the eyes of others mirroring your Love and Gratitude. Just as you created a bridge between your mirrored image and the true Self, you will also create a powerful connection between you and each being you encounter.

Imagine – you will be creating a world of waking Love and Gratitude by mirroring the Divine within YOU.

~ FOUR ~
Living LaRGe

Water is intelligent, and no matter how toxic or polluted it may become, will return to a state of purity when treated with Love, Respect and Gratitude. Surface tension will change so toxins within each water droplet fall away returning the water crystal to a state of purity, beauty and symmetry.

Consider focusing on Love, Respect, and Gratitude as you drink each glass of water. Let these feelings flow through you as this blessed water floods your body's cells with purity, beauty and symmetry.

Remember the body of Earth, like you, is approx. 70% water, so project Love, Respect and Gratitude across her surface, as well. Close your eyes and imagine toxins releasing from each drop of water covering Earth's body, returning her to a perfect state of health and vitality.

Joyfully receive this harmonious state of beauty and perfection. This purity will naturally flow through humanity, as well. All water holds an energetic signature whether walking, waking, or still. Remember – you are walking water, connected by resonance with every other body of water on the planet . . . be it person, puddle or pond.

Living LaRGe is an easy-to-remember phrase for connecting to the power, promise, and extensive effect of Love, Respect and Gratitude as a healing force for our planetary bodies of water. Shift your perspective of water to honor its interconnected-ness and fluid state of being as a mirror of humanity. By living LaRGe – Love, Respect, and Gratitude – you will clear, seal and heal our waters in Divine time for all generations to thrive on Mother Earth.

~ FIVE ~
A Bridge to Peace

One morning I woke, pulling myself from a deep immersion in a feeling of Grey. During the night I dreamed of children, torn and tattered by the effects of war and silently crying for a ray of light – for a beam to chase away the darkness and lift them into hope.

As I pondered this dream experience, I realized there is only one war – the war that wages within ourselves, a battle between heart and mind to direct our physical reality. Once we surrender to NOW, using Gratitude to guide us to a state of Love, then Peace reigns within the Self and will, by nature, spill into our waking reality – both near and far.

At the heart of war I see resistance, in whatever form this may appear. It is our highest nature signaling to us that our thoughts, beliefs, values, attitudes, words, goals and/or actions are OUT OF ALIGNMENT with our pure state of Being.

Let us then use this resistance – this tugging, gnawing, twisting, burning sensation within – to ignite a process that will quickly return us to center, to our higher path.

Remembering war begins with-in, let us establish peace between the mind and heart by imagining a bridge. This bridge spans the distance between the mind and heart and opens a path for reconciling the being–doing–having aspects of Life.

Here is an amazingly simple, powerfully effective process that, when applied with intent, will create a state of Peace, Grace, and Openness within every moment. This Process is inspired by Dr. Emoto's formula of two parts Gratitude and one part Love and is a powerful tool I personally use to gracefully move through moments of growth, change or choice.

Ready?

Ok, here goes:

Imagine resistance is signaling a course correction. Now:

1. Give Thanks
2. Ask Love
3. Go Gratitude

Perhaps this sounds too simple?

This is the beauty of the process, and why it is so easy to use on a daily basis. Let's quickly explore the finer points of this process.

Step one: Give Thanks
By acknowledging that the moment is a gift, The Present, and is designed by YOU as an opportunity to learn, release, and

re-center, you are opening an opportunity to return to the heart of the matter.

A short mantra may be: 'I AM thankful for NOW.'

Step Two: Ask Love

Go to your heart, allowing each and every cell within your body to radiate Love while simultaneously asking, 'What is my message? What is the gift Now brings to me? What habit/ belief/fear am I ready to release gaining insight, wisdom, and direction?

A short mantra may be: 'I AM Love's Messenger.'

Step Three: Go Gratitude!

As you are now aware of patterns creating resistance in your life, you are prepared to tap into Gratitude as a guide for your next step, using the wisdom Love has given you as a source to draw from. Allow yourself to trust what your heart has shared and go forward in Gratitude.

A short mantra may be: 'I AM waking Gratitude.'

Now, you may be wondering 'How does this work?'

Quite simply, you are building a bridge between your Heart-Mind . . . one that will continue to grow in strength, speed, and span as you make the journey between choice and effect, an event simply called NOW.

As you use this technique, it will quickly become a habit, then a Mastered Skill, and eventually a State of Being. By quickening your ability to listen, learn, and receive, you stand before all doors of possibility, as a living, breathing Master of Love and Gratitude.

This three step process will quickly flow into a singular state of being, that of Peace. Beyond the physical bodily signals of resistance, there are other ways to roll through this process within the body. Let nature be your guide, as well as serendipitous events and divinely timed memories that flash an opportunity to view your past anew.

As today rolls on you may find yourself confronted with the reality of war, whether it be across our lands, thundering in our homes or present in our hearts. Let us give thanks to know there is Peace – and that Peace begins with ME.

As you begin to peacefully translate your heart's thoughts, wisdom and intuition, you will be keenly aware of the effects on your reality and of those around you. You draw inspiration from source and serve as an earthly messenger who willingly strives to be excellent in all communications of the heart, spirit, soul, mind and body.

Within each of us is an innocent child, one who remembers every answer, who must forget what time has erased and let Love be the guide. Just for today – let us be the Peace we seek, by bridging heart to mind through Love and Gratitude.

Chief Seattle, who shares that the longest journey one will make is from the mind to the heart, offers this bit of wisdom: "Gratitude is when memory is stored in the heart and not in the mind. All things are bound together. All things connect." A bridge to Peace indeed.

~ SIX ~
A Serving of Gratitude

Imagine, for one day, you are responsible for solely completing every aspect of each task before you. You may be required to drive your trash to the dump, deliver mail to intended recipients, drill, refine, transport, store AND pump your own gas. Perhaps you will grow, shelf, and grind wheat to bake and serve bread . . . Whew! We have yet to address power for lights, water for drinking, or schooling for children.

These services, and myriad of others, are provided by a heavenly host of earthly angels who show up each day to serve and support our daily lives. It is often easy to forget the valuable time afforded us by those who take care of the "little details" – who show up to do their part and take their place in the great circle of Life.

As a matter of living, occasionally long lines, hold times, out-of-stock items or a change in price will create an inconvenient wait, urging the practice of patience, or may altogether re-arrange anticipated plans. By shifting to Gratitude you will begin to focus on the gift of the experience rather than the challenge at hand.

As you flow into the perfection of the moment, take a deep breath and release. Breathe again deeply, this time releasing all resistance to present circumstances while seeking a way to express Gratitude Now. This choice to shift into Gratitude opens a multitude of opportunities to infect others with this source-force energy, while centering you in an empowered state of creation.

Consciously choosing to express Gratitude will aid other people's ability to experience Joy through the power of appreciation and will flood you with an instantaneous feeling of peace and goodwill.

Now, imagine how many, many others will benefit from a simple 'Thank You' or a grateful glance. As this energetic message is passed along, an ever-widening circle of influence is being created by you – one flowing through Love and Gratitude.

So it is in all matters of service. Simply shift to Gratitude, follow a path to origin of source while giving thanks every step of the way. Breathe deeply, release and seek to reflect your Love and Gratitude for all services you receive. Go Gratitude!

~ SEVEN ~
Keep what's worth keeping and return the rest to Love

In order to flow through Now in a state of health and perfection, our bodies will go through a release – old thoughts, habits, feelings, and physical materials will be returned to Source, purified by loving intent leaving space for possibilities to manifest that resonate with current states of being.

Use this secret to clear, seal and heal the body:

Close your eyes. Imagine your heart center, a meeting point between the four chambers hosting an eternal flame. This flame, this light, this pulsing point of universal connection gives life, spark, and energetic presence for Love to BE. Now imagine this light is reflected within the core of every cell within your being. Let this light pulse, play and dance by your mere attentions, expressing Gratitude knowing Divinity is present within every facet of your physical being.

Now return to your heart light. Imagine this light beginning to spin in unison with Gratitude, creating a vortex. Now expand this vortex as a two-sided funnel. Open on top, flowing to a central core, then expanding again on the underside to create a passage way for Will, thoughts, feelings, and physical material to move through.

Now imagine this funnel reflected in every living, loving cell within your body. As you witness this sparkling universe being revealed, take a deep, cleansing breath. Let this breath fan the flames of Love, health, vitality, and perfection within your body.

With each breath, witness the presence of magnetism and gravity at play, creating a whirling, swirling flow of Love and Gratitude through every particle of living light. As this flow gains force by your direct attention, consciously command this vortex to transmute past into present, releasing old habits, thoughts, desires, and physical materials that have served their purpose.

Give thanks for these teachers, for their wisdom brings you to NOW!

As time passes through the infinite, You remember to follow this simple guide: Keep what's worth keeping and return the rest to Love. With each beat of time, every pulse of light sublime, you will be creating space for Now possibilities to flow through you.

Let this flow create a state of perfection, a Divine Alignment with all that IS. As you feel clear, give thanks for remembering the Universe within. Seal this journey by returning to Love and accept you are Now healed.

As above, So below
So within, So without
As the Universe, so the Soul

~ EIGHT ~
Discipline of Gratitude

At the root of the word Discipline is Disciple, defined by Merriam-Webster as "one who accepts and assists in spreading the doctrines of another". And the definition of doctrine? Quite simply – teaching or instruction.

So what does it mean to spread the doctrine of another?

To live what others have given you – be it information, wisdom, or example.

Essentially, by living Love and Gratitude, we exponentially increase our creative abilities by disciplining ourselves to re-member, honor, and reflect the gifts others have given us. We become disciples of living Love and Gratitude.

Now, in order to fully embrace, emulate and exemplify the gifts of others, a present awareness is required. How do we cultivate a present awareness of lessons learned, insight gained, and methods mastered? Express Gratitude for persons in your life – whether directly connected or admired from afar – who have profoundly influenced you.

In short – Remember to express Gratitude for those who assist You in being YOU.

As you return Gratitude, your mind-body-spirit connects with the presence of lessons shared and infuses Now with energetic support for current endeavors.

Here is an enlightening exercise, a whole-life approach to returning Gratitude for the disciplines present within you:

Look at the Wheel of Transformation (p. 157), and remember a person who has directly affected your growth from each area, whose example, wisdom, or presence profoundly influences your life. Re-member, this may be someone who guided you directly, an author whose words released floods of 'ah-ha!'s and knowing, a sibling, parent – perhaps an artist conveying truth so eloquently you knew it was created just for YOU.

Now give thanks to each person, connecting heart to heart, for their attention, presence, and impact upon your life. You may also choose to express Gratitude by letter, phone call, or even a timely visit. You will know which methods best suits you.

By consciously expressing Gratitude, you seal a connection between each of you, creating a present moment awareness of shared time, talents, and treasures. This discipline of Gratitude will magnify and reflect the efforts of others, enhancing your ability to spread the messages shared between you. You become a living disciple of Love and Gratitude.

Additionally, using the Wheel of Transformation will build an earthly organization of universal assets, confirming you are surrounded by Masters from all areas of Life. This present awareness allows you to flow with the Go, as you are energetically aligned with Masters existing throughout all time. Remember, every student has a teacher, every teacher a Master, every Master a discipline. Master the discipline of Gratitude and all doors will open to you.

~ NINE ~
Good Night, Gratitude

A simple, powerfully effective practice for aligning with the Laws of Attraction is to give thanks Now for what IS, knowing this will prompt the Universe to continue delivering that which you appreciate most. What is the Law of Attraction? Quite simply: Like attracts Like.

Consider this:

Oprah Winfrey, following a prompt from Sarah Ban Breathnach's book Simple Abundance, began keeping a nightly Gratitude journal. Oprah credits this one practice as a major life changing experience, enhancing and supporting her ability to be a conscious creator saying, "Keep a grateful journal. Every night, list five things that you are grateful for. What it will begin to do is change your perspective of your day and your life."

You see, by recording your "gratefuls", you will flood your body with serotonin, a neurotransmitter that promotes relaxation, restful sleep and a sense of well being. Imagine waking each day from a peaceful sleep, after immersing your mind-body-spirit in a gentle bath of Gratitude. You will surely experience a shift in energetic perspective, present moment awareness and magnetically charge your ability to create a Joyful day.

In order to enhance this journaling practice, consider these three ways to intimately expand the recording of your Gratitude's:

1.   As your write, use "feeling" words to vividly describe the emotions associated with this gift of Gratitude Allow this emotional connection with Gratitude to enhance, magnify, and radiate throughout your being–ness.

2.   Consider a recent moment of resistance. Let this memory flow lovingly through Gratitude. As you release into the perfection of this experience, record your (k)new found perspective giving thanks for quickened wisdom and the gift of growth as you gracefully move through daily challenges.

3.   Give thanks for future possibilities, opportunities, and planned events. By giving thanks Now you draw there to here by energetically aligning your Self with your intentions.

Remember, by outwardly expressing your inward appreciation, you create a written history of time reflecting all that is joyfully sublime in your world, while cultivating a discipline for viewing life through Love and Gratitude.

Go Gratitude!

A GO GRATITUDE CONSPIRACY

Imagine lying on your back, lazily gazing into a star filled night, waving your ankles and toes through a swirling pool of warm, comforting water.

This is me, midnight, New Years 2003, at a sea-side resort in San Diego, drifting in and out of consciousness, floating in the pure bliss of Being. Suddenly, a call reverberated through my entire being, interrupting my hypnotic reverie, whispering, "It's time to Go!"

Quite comfortable and prepared to rest for some time, I closed my eyes and waved off the prompting.

Once again, this time clear, commanding and distinct, I heard, "It's time to GO!"

'Ok, Ok, I'm on my way.'

As I put on my shoes, I took a few moments to revel in the blissful atmosphere, appreciate the stars over San Diego, the ebb and flow of the sea and the promise of a New Year. Little did I know that moment would bring me to the love of my life who was sitting outside his room, just across from me, also under the spell of the stars and waves.

This inner voice, drawing me toward my destiny and pulling

me from desire to reality, opened a door of possibility – one leading to my partner, my soul-mate, and the co-creator of Go Gratitude. In essence, this message asked me to Go Now. Go to Love and soon to Go Gratitude . . .

Today, it is my pleasure to introduce a silent partner who also brings Go Gratitude to you – a brilliant Internet veteran, mass communications specialist and the Love of my life, Ken Herbert.

We met serendipitously, on New Year's Day 2003, in San Diego. Our timing was absolutely Divine. Ken, who lived in Oregon and I, from Arizona, both found our way to the exact same spot at precisely the same time, under the heavens, where we talked all night and felt an instant soul-reconnection.

So compelling was our connection that it was only a short time before he moved to Arizona, where we both realized the Pacific Northwest was calling us and we made our journey here. His office now sits above mine in our two-story home where we live, love, laugh and co-create together. I lovingly refer to him as, 'The Man Upstairs.'

In order to truly give you a view of who's creating Go Gratitude, it seems fitting to share our story and, as promised, a Go Gratitude conspiracy . . .

Did I say conspiracy?

Absolutely! Do you know that to conspire means "To breathe together in harmony"?

Though this word is commonly used to imply under-handed, dark doings, at its roots, it is simply describing two or more hearts gathered to breathe in shared time. Wow!

Beginning with Ken and I, quickly flowing through hearts and minds world wide, we now count an astounding collection of co-conspirators as we create our world wide wave of Gratitude!

Imagine... each breath we exhale, swirling mists of intentioned time, immerses our air, rain, clouds, oceans, rivers, Yes! – all bodies of water – in Love and Gratitude. Including the one you are sitting in Now. (Your body, of course!)

Allow me Now to share some of what makes he and me We ... *and how this relates to YOU!*

I fell in Love with the timbre of his voice, his ever-present inquisitive nature, and true belief in Self. In fact, to this day, Ken is one of the most inspiring people I am honored to share time with. He is dedicated to his craft, always seeking to refine his level of discipline and genuinely supports and celebrates others to excel, as well.

One of his inspired creations, called Dream Quest, is a program designed to assist the process of thriving while living in one's passions. It is a comprehensive, in-depth course that requires one to first look inside, then to discover ways to apply the gifts, skills, and unique personality held within to create the life of one's dreams.

Ken had created the perfect tool for me. Truly.

By nature, I am a seeker, a voracious reader and my interests roll all over creation. I had considered a million and one (a modest number) crazy ventures along the way, though each one seemed to smolder as quickly as it had ignited. I often realized my daily commitment to required tasks was more than my spontaneous nature was willing to support. I knew that my chosen venture–calling would have to be something universal yet personal to keep my interest.

So Ken passed a secret to me, the essence of Dream Quest, and one that daily changes my life. What was this life-changing, ever-so-powerful, simple and yet complex piece of wisdom?

Know Yourself.

Yes! Know Your 'Self.'

Be willing to listen to the heart's desires beating within – and to trust, while also creating and allowing the necessary plans, structures and opportunities to reveal themselves in order to fulfill the heart's desires.

Now, trusting was something that came slowly to me. As a young child, being an Empath, I cultivated two survival skills. One, how to please and two, to never fully trust anyone. This method worked marginally, just enough to create an illusion of effectiveness . . . until Ken came along.

You see, a few years before we met, he wrote out a recipe, an order if you will, for his perfect Soul Mate. (See the section following this one: Soulmate Manifesto) When he revealed this to me just recently, I cried to see myself written on the pages of time.

Only there's one catch – Ken called up my highest Self, and every day, every moment we are together this is what he sees in me. This requires me to look inside, to listen, and be my highest Self – to rise to the occasion and to be the quintessential ME.

This is where Go Gratitude entered our lives.

Just about the time I took my 42 day retreat, I was bursting at the seams with Love, knowledge, a sincere desire to serve and no structure for making this happen. I decided enough! and cocooned myself on our little piece of heaven for 6 weeks to explore, reveal, and create a (k)new Stacey.

Now, you may have questioned the spelling of '(k)new,' asking 'Is this a typo'?

Absolutely! An intentional one, of course.

You see, what I realized during this retreat is truth is present in every moment, our spirits are connected to all things and it is simply our task to remember what time has forgotten. So new is really (k)new. Plus, it's a fabulous way to re-arrange old perceptions – a powerful tool during this time of Global transformation, to be sure.

So back to Gratitude . . .

Once I had connected the symbol and the essence of its message, I began cultivating a discipline of Gratitude. Each day, waking to follow this dream, I was thrilled to gather, collect and organize information plus trust, trust, trust my heart.

Think about it . . . a world wide wave of Gratitude?
big, Big, BIG to be sure!

Trust preceded each step I took, and I remember feeling a building desire and commitment to continue, consistent support from the universe and my eyes beaming each time I told someone about my dream – even to those who returned confused, dazed gazes. (There were a lot to begin with, trust me!)

Throughout the eight months time leading up to the launch of Go Gratitude, I followed numerous promptings, intuitive callings, and accepted a great deal of universal assistance, including Ken's unwavering belief, intuitive coaching and savvy approach to Internet communications. Thank You, Love. Thank you for being You and Loving me for Me.

Now, are you ready for a little secret?

Go Gratitude launched on November 21, 2005 and 42 days later (42 [k]new views on Gratitude), on Jan. 1, 2006, Ken and I celebrated our third anniversary.

This is our gift to one another. To live, love, breathe and be in Gratitude each and every waking day of our lives. To weave our skills, passions, and unique attributes to create peace in our home, Love in our hearts and Heaven on Earth.

It is our honor to share our lives with YOU. It is by your reflections, efforts, and inspired ideas that we know our time is well spent and our endeavors worth while. What a gift you have given us. Thank you.

In truth, this Love story is about us, all of US, who dare to listen to our hearts, to follow our dreams, and believe that together we are One. One heart, One Mind, One planet. So, in our heart-minds, Ken and I are conspiring with YOU to create a world-wide wave of Gratitude.

As this wave flows across land and sea, we are activating seeds of abundance that lay dormant – these are our Divine inheritance, our birthright – which will spring forth to create joy, peace, harmony and a world overflowing with Love and Gratitude!

All together Now . . .

Go Gratitude!

SOUL MATE MANIFESTO

I see a new and exciting person entering my life's experience. This person is a beautiful female who vibrates in harmony with what I am wanting. She is spiritual in the sense that she knows who she is and believes that all things are possible and is moving in the same limitless direction that I am.

She has a wonderful sense of humor and appreciates mine as we bring out the best feelings in each other when we are together. She has a sense of adventure and a willingness to try new things. She is curious by nature and loves learning, experiencing and experimenting.

She is honest with her feelings and dealings with me and others. She is positive, upbeat and happy. She is a joy to be around and I feel wonderful to be with her. She has her own mind and is independent emotionally and financially.

She is vibrant and healthy-she literally glows with energy and enthusiasm. She believes in herself and believes in me. Her sublime gentle nature is a grace that makes all our interactions smooth, natural and effortless. We support each other in our life's mission and I feel like a king when I am with her and she feels like my queen. We are able to speak for hours with each other, while at the same time being able to give each other space when we want it.

She loves to travel and has a great appreciation for the beauty, serenity, and grandeur of nature. She really feels like a soul-mate, sharing a like-mind and soul. She is full of life and reminds me of the power of love. There is a magnet-like pull that draws us together. There is definitely a strong sense of physical attraction and at the same time the attraction extends beyond the physical and into the emotional, mental and spiritual side as well. We are a perfect match and are in harmony on all levels. She is a growth seeking being and we enjoy growing together and learning from one another.

I see myself sharing my life with this beautiful, loving, fun, supportive, honest, gentle, spiritual, intelligent soul-mate. When I am with her, I feel alive and strong, more of my best self. I feel the great possibility of all things. Talking with her is like talking to myself for her thoughts are my thoughts. We are one and we are in harmony. Our relationship grows through love and great joy and a desire to always expand the limits of our beliefs. We want to experience all the richness that life has to offer. This life is a wonderful adventure/creation and we expectantly look forward to each new day.

I have made space for this special lady in my life – someone of like mind and heart. I feel her definitely being attracted to me as I am writing this. We will meet and there will be joy and excitement in our meeting. She will see what I'm doing and support it wholeheartedly as I will be committed to assisting her in fulfilling her life's purpose.

Ken Herbert – 2000

ACKNOWLEDGEMENTS
MY GRATITUDE

When I heard the Hopi teaching, "We are the Ones we've been waiting for," my heart sang a song of Gratitude. Ever since I was a young girl I've felt an insatiable yearning to make a difference in the world.

Always a believer, I have followed many a path in pursuit of this goal – and have been blessed by the guidance, presence, and example of Masters from every area and discipline of Life. So when I heard this message, this clarion call, a thought struck me.

'We are all Masters – as we so choose. So choose Now.'

From that moment on, I sensed an ever-present connection to Source and a deep feeling of belonging. Rather than being a lone crusader, I realized myself to be in the company of living Masters – some who remember, and some who will remember. These Masters, also known as visionaries, artists, writers, friends and family alike, have assisted me in bringing Go Gratitude to you.

I thank first of all Ken Herbert, my Soul Mate, partner in creation and best friend. Without his skill for project management, Go Gratitude might be a dusty collection of doodled ideas in forgotten notebooks.

Loving Gratitude goes to my two Mothers – the one who gave me Life through Love and the one who gave me the Love of my Life – thank for your grace, creativity and willingness to simply listen. To my Aunt DeeVie, whose name means Of Life, thank you for assisting my transition from sleeping caterpillar to joyful Butterfly.

Many thanks and much appreciation goes to Carol Hansen Grey for her skills as a graphic artist, social activist, and friend. I gave Carol the structure, she gave the Gratitude symbol a glowing countenance.

I also acknowledge Robert Evans, and his fabulous team of creative mavens at Pass Along Concepts. At our first meeting, Robert's eyes beamed with excitement, brightening every corner of the room. He instantly caught the vision and daily magnifies it. Many others along the way have directly affected the manner, method and timing of how Go Gratitude came to be, including Julie Jordan Scott, Steve Marsden, Sheila Finkelstein, Kathy Kochevar, and R. Scott Curry. Thank you for being YOU.

Finally, a big, Big, BIG thank you to the participants of Go Gratitude for sharing your intimate experiences, life changing stories, and 'ah-ha!' moments. It is through you this experiment truly springs to life, allowing multitudes of others to enjoy these living, loving gifts of Gratitude, too.

Go Gratitude!

RESOURCES

Barbara Marx Hubbard ~ www.evolve.org

Barry Carter ~ www.SubtleEnergies.com/ormus/index.htm

Carmen Colombo ~ www.wowzone.com/wowintro.htm

Carol Hansen Grey ~ www.CarolHansenGrey.com

Celia Fenn ~ www.StarChildAscension.org

Daily Dose of Gratitude ~
http://groups.yahoo.com/groupDailyDose_Gratitude

Gillian MacBeth-Louthan ~ www.TheQuantumAwakening.com

Gratitude Ceremony ~ www.GratitudeCeremony.com

Gregg Braden ~ www.GreggBraden.com

Jennifer Hoffman ~ www.UrielHeals.com

Julie Jordan Scott ~ www.GoGratitude.com/julie.html

Kathy Kochevar ~ www.EarthandSkyMandalas.com

lightSOURCE ~ www.GoGratitude.com/sacred-geometry.html

Master Kirael ~ www.Kirael.com/GoGratitude

Pass Along Concepts ~ www.PassAlongConcepts.com

Sandy Grason ~ www.SandyGrason.com

Sheila Finkelstein ~ www.Eteletours.com/ptpintro.html

Spiritus Sanctus ~ www.SpiritusSanctus.com

Wild Divine ~ www.GoGratitude.com/wild-divine.html

Wingmakers ~ www.WantToKnow.info/wingmakers2

Yoga of Alignment ~ www.theYogaOfAlignment.com

Downloads:

The Master Key System by Charles F. Haanel ~
www.GoGratitude.com/masterkey-ebook.html

3D animated Go Gratitude screensaver ~
http://all7.com/gratitude.htm

ABOUT THE AUTHOR

As an Intuitive Healer and Empath with a passion for asking revealing questions, Stacey Robyn sees life from the inside out.

Her creative experience in photography together with a life long study of visual archetypes and spatial relationships has fostered a fascination with discovering the patterns of creation reflected in every facet of life.

By combining these interests with creative writing and her history of social activism, the author has brought Go Gratitude from conception to realization.

Stacey Robyn lives in the Pacific Northwest.